W9-BRO-302

Quilt Designs
from Down East

Quilt
Designs
from Down East

24 Projects for
Beginner to Advanced Stitchers

Patricia A. Aho

To my parents, Henry and Phyllis Benner, who encouraged my curiosity and permitted me to explore any avenue that caught my fancy. They taught me that a sense of humor will get you through the most difficult situation.

Special thanks to Gary for his encouragement and tolerance.

Text copyright © 1991 by Patricia A. Aho
Photographs © 1991 by Richard Procopio
ISBN 0-89272-283-5

Design by Mary Jennings
Color separations prepared by Four Color Imports
Printed and Bound at Capital City Press, Montpelier, Vt.

5   4   3   2   1

Down East Books

CONTENTS

PREFACE

Twenty-two years ago I attended a quilting class offered at the local YMCA. The instructor never told us about quilting needles and thread, nor did she mention cutting lines or seam lines. She did bring patterns, and she told us about one-quarter-inch seams. Despite this sketchy introduction, I was hooked. I completed a quilt top by hand using scrap materials left from sewing for my children. I have certainly done better work since then, but that quilt remains one of my favorites.

Over the years I have myself taught quilting classes and learned new techniques. My teaching methods have been altered and reshaped. I started as a purist, doing everything by hand. I allowed my pupils the choice of hand or machine piecing, but never myself. I now use a sewing machine for some patch construction, but still prefer doing handwork.

Quilting has taken me down new roads—both literally and figuratively. I stop anywhere there is quilting to be viewed or discussed. My mind spins with ideas for new patterns and old. It is impossible for me to venture near cloth without visualizing a new project, and my fabric supply runneth over.

This book is the culmination of a dream. It comes after encouraging words and a little prodding from family and friends. The designs reflect my love for the outdoors and for the area where I live. They may appeal to you somewhat differently, for quilting designs have a way of becoming personal to the individual quilter. Their simple, abstract shapes beckon each of us to read our own meaning and memories into them.

Modern-day quilters follow the creative tradition of their predecessors when they team a pattern with their own chosen colors and fabrics. Each combination has a distinctively individual look and becomes a reflection of the quilter who created it.

Wonderful memories kept popping into my head as I worked on the designs for this book, and I've decided to share those recollections as I introduce each project. These motifs will also conjure up memories for you, I am sure, for a quilt in the making warms the heart as surely as a quilt on the bed warms the body.

A NOTE BEFORE YOU START

This design collection offers patterns for quilters at all levels of expertise. I've included simple patterns such as Maple Leaf for beginners, while others—North Star, for example—will challenge more seasoned stitchers.

Although the pattern instructions suggest specific projects for each patch, please don't assume that you are limited to only those combinations. Most of the patchwork squares can be adapted to other uses, and will work equally well on a pillow, a tote bag, a wall hanging, or combined into a quilt. If you would like a different motif on your windsock or a different quilting design on your potpourri-filled coasters than what I used, by all means improvise!

For example, you might want to alternate squares of North Wind and Snowflake for a lovely quilt. Or you could enlarge the shell quilting design in Heaven Scent and team it with Bouncing Buoys or Compass for a small throw.

By combining components from two or more of the items in this book, you can create whatever object catches your fancy.

The only designs that do *not* lend themselves readily to small projects are Tall Pine Tree, Delectable Mountains, Stormbound, and Mountains, Lakes, and Sea. However, you can always make larger finished items with these designs by increasing the number of patches used or adding wider borders.

THE EYE OF THE NEEDLE (AND OTHER TERRIFIC TOOLS)

Needles and pins,
Needles and pins,
Add cloth, thread, and scissors,
And quilting begins.

Quilting is one-fourth knowledge and three-fourths experience, so don't become discouraged if your first attempts are less than perfect.

One thing helpful to quality quilting is the equipment in the quilter's sewing basket. There are endless gadgets, but only a few tools are absolutely necessary.

The Necessary Tools

- *Needles* are very important. Always use quilting needles, which are made especially for quilting and are shorter and slimmer than needles intended for other handwork. They range from size 7 to 12, with the higher number indicating the smaller needle. Quilting needles will seem minute at first, but soon you will find it difficult to maneuver anything larger.

- *Straight pins* are needed for pinning the pieces together. Sizes 5 and 6 are best because they are sharp and thin and won't leave holes in the fabric.

- *Quilting thread* comes in a variety of colors, although it is not imperative to match thread color to the fabric being used. I use only two colors: white and off-white. (Except that I did work the Snowflake quilting design in blue for this book, so it would photograph better.)

   The important thing to keep in mind concerning thread is how much to put on your needle. Never cut thread longer than 18 to 20 inches. Longer pieces tend to fray or knot.

- There are several types of *thimble* on the market. I prefer the leather one that covers my finger to the second knuckle. Often quilters will use a thimble on each hand—one for pushing the needle through the layers of material and the other, placed on the opposite hand, to "feel" the needle coming through the back.

- A *measuring tool* of some kind is necessary. A ruler is fine. I also have a quilter's T-square and an 18-inch ruler that is 6 inches wide and has quarter-inch markings.

- *Beeswax* is handy. Pulling the thread through beeswax before sewing with it helps prevent tangles and strengthens the thread.

- Have *markers* with your quilting notions. These are used to trace around templates and for transferring quilting designs. I use a pencil when it's possible. There are quilt markers that will disappear when rubbed with a damp cloth, and even one that vanishes on its own after a few hours. Never use a ballpoint pen! The results could be disastrous.

- *Templates* may be purchased ready-made or cut as needed from sheets of template plastic. Precut plastic or metal ones are available in all sizes and shapes. Either of these selections gives a template that can be used indefinitely. Since many patterns call for common-sized templates, quilters frequently opt for these standard shapes.

   A cardboard cereal box cut to size serves the purpose well. However, cardboard templates will have to be replaced as they wear out.

   Medium-weight sandpaper was my choice of template material for many years. It has the advantage of staying put when placed on the fabric. Glueing it to one side of a plastic template works well also.

- Perhaps the most important tool in a quilter's kit is a good pair of *scissors*. They should be kept exclusively for cutting cloth. An old pair can be used for cutting paper, plastic, and, yes, even batting. Fabric shears should be for cloth only.

These are the bare necessities. Many other time-saving accouterments are available, and they are useful and fun to work with but not necessary for a superior result.

SAY WHAT?
A GLOSSARY OF QUILTING TERMS

Many things we encounter in our lives have a language all their own. Quilting is no exception. Here are some of the most useful terms. At first they might seem confusing, but soon they will become very familiar.

Appliqué: The layering of one piece of fabric upon another. An appliqué design is made up of many pieces, which are stitched to a foundation block.

Backing: The bottom layer of a quilting project.

Batting: The filler used as an interlining between the quilt top and the backing. Several types are available. Cotton requires close lines of quilting—every half inch—to hold the batting together. Wool is warm, and lighter than cotton, but tends to be expensive. Polyester, because of the way it is woven, only needs to be quilted every four to six inches. It also launders well.

Bias: The diagonal weave of fabric. The fabric will stretch across the bias. When fabric is cut on the bias, it will accommodate curves.

Binding: Finishing the raw edges of a quilting project. In one method, the backing is made larger than the quilt top, folded over and brought forward over the edge of the top layer, and blind-stiched in place. Another method is to encase the raw edges in bias tape made of matching or contrasting material. The top and back may also be turned in to each other and stitched together.

Block: A design unit of the quilting project. A number of blocks make up a quilt or wall hanging.

Border: A frame of fabric stitched around the center of a quilting project. Often one or more borders are added to achieve the desired final dimensions.

Grain: Fabric has a definite grain. The "straight of the goods" runs exactly across and exactly up and down the fabric, while the bias (see above) runs diagonally.

Interlining: The middle layer of a quilting project. It may be batting or a lightweight blanket. It provides warmth and body.

Lattice strips: Equal-sized strips of fabric that form a grid and are used to frame the blocks of a quilt top or wall hanging.

Marking: A means of putting the quilting design on the quilt in preparation for quilting.

Miter: A means of turning a ninety-degree corner with a straight strip of fabric. Mitering gives the most professional look to finished quilt corners.

Patch: Synonymous with "block." It is a square divided into parts that have been stitched together—in other words, a patchwork square.

Patchwork: A project that has been stitched together from pieces cut into shapes such as triangles, squares, diamonds, and the like, and sewed together into a design.

Piece: A segment of cloth used in a quilting project (noun). To join these segments together to make a block or patch (verb).

Running stitch: The stitch used for basting, hand piecing, and decorative quilting.

Sandwich: The result produced after layering the backing, the interlining, and the top. These three layers are basted together in preparation for quilting.

Square: A patchwork square is the same as a quilt patch.

Top: The top layer of the quilting project. It may be pieced, appliquéd, embroidered, etc.

Quilt: A cover made of three layers—a top, an interlining, and a back—held together with decorative stitching (noun). Securing these three layers together with decorative stitching done either by hand or by machine (verb).

Quilt frame: A wooden stretcher or a large hoop that holds a quilt taut during quilting.

BRING ME A RAINBOW: SELECTING COLORS

After deciding on a pattern, the next step is choosing colors. This should be done with great care, especially on a large project. The choice of colors often makes or breaks a project.

Color creates mood. If a cheerful mood is desired, the colors should be bright and gay. Primary colors convey this message, and they are especially good for children's projects.

Victorian combinations take on a more subdued, softer appearance. These often have a dark, sophisticated look.

Country colors, on the other hand, tend to be more of a medium value, with variations of the primary colors.

A monochromatic color scheme can be extremely effective. This is when one color is used in many different shades and patterns. The Village Green design in this book is an example of a monochromatic look.

Sometimes the design itself establishes the colors to be used. Many of the patterns in this book lend themselves to certain colors. A purple ocean would never do, while gray is always a safe choice for the rocks in an ocean scene.

For a two-color pattern, it is wise to use a light and a dark color. If both fabrics are close in color value, the effect is boring. One color should be used in a larger quantity.

There are a few rules to observe when shopping for prints. When using more than one, choose prints of varying sizes. Large prints will not work well in small designs. If stripes catch your fancy, be aware that they need care when cutting; the stripes need to run in the right direction.

In the past, the quilter was often limited in the choice of colors and patterns by the availability of fabrics. Today's quilter has unlimited combinations from which to choose. Since color and pattern affect the overall look of a project, it pays to take care and time in making a final choice. It is a shame to put hours and money into any project that will not bring joy to the creator for many years to come.

When searching for cloth, remember that warm colors (reds, yellows, oranges) are cheerful and stimulating and they "advance" in the design. By the same token, the cool colors (blues, greens, purples) recede in a design and are calming and restful. It is possible to combine warm and cool colors as long as they harmonize.

Always keep in mind where a project is to be placed. Any design should blend with its surroundings.

When I'm choosing fabric for a new undertaking, I start by deciding what color or colors will dominate. The next step is to find a pleasing fabric in that predominant hue. If there is to be more than one prevalent color, I often look for a fabric that has one of the colors in its background and the other color as part of its print. Then I search for another print that has those colors in the opposite relationship—the background color of the first fabric becomes the print color of the second. I place these bolts side by side, step back several feet (as if viewing a painting), and observe them. If I am pleased with the way they look together under these circumstances, then I know I will be satisfied when they are stitched together in a block. If more than two fabrics are called for, proceed with this same method.

After all is said and done, the most important rule of all is to select colors you like, and you won't fail. It helps to take a friend along for moral support and advice—and going out for lunch can also help ease the strain.

FUNDAMENTAL FABRICS

When shopping for fabric for a quilting project, there are a few considerations to keep in mind. The most important is the type of material. When making a quilt or other large endeavor, buy only the best-quality fabric. Sometimes the temptation to save a few dollars looms large; do not succumb to it. You may save money in the beginning, but somewhere along the line, more than savings will be lost.

It takes untold hours to complete a large project, and it should give pleasure for many years. Cheap material often shrinks. It may not wear well, and sometimes the colors run. Most important of all, that look of quality is not there. If saving money is a priority, it is better to wait for a sale than settle for fabric of lesser quality.

Rather than compromise a first project by purchasing inferior material because the creator is not confident of the final result, it's better to start with a smaller project, such as a pillow or tote bag.

Most quilted items should be made of calico or good-quality cotton. Both are durable and fine enough to be easy to quilt. They should be closely woven and soft, not stiff.

Gingham looks wonderful with calico, especially when fashioning baby objects, but it has a tendency to ravel and for this reason should probably be avoided.

It is perfectly all right to use cotton blends, although purists prefer only 100 percent cotton. However, when making anything larger than a pillow, I don't recommend combining all-cotton with cotton-blend materials. They do not mellow at the same rate. ("Mellow" has a much nicer sound than "fade.") Cotton will mellow with time. That's what gives an antique quilt its charm. And since cotton blends do not fade at the same rate as pure cotton, that gorgeous quilt could take on a look that is less than desirable. Use one or the other, but not a combination of the two.

Heavier materials, such as corduroy, are fine for piecing or appliqué but are too thick for quilting and should be made into a tied coverlet instead.

Before using any fabric, wash and dry it. Most of today's fabrics do not shrink, nor do the colors run, but there is always the outside chance that one will. Therefore, it is better to be safe than sorry.

I usually purchase a bit more than I need for a given task because I like having leftovers for future endeavors. I've even been known to buy cloth just because I liked it, with no particular project in mind at the time. In fact, when I die, someone is going to have a grand time going through my stash of fabric. My husband is taking odds that I am going to take the prize that a certain bumper sticker proclaims: THE ONE WITH THE MOST FABRIC WHEN SHE DIES WINS!

SIMPLE STITCHES
AND SECURE SEAMS

As a general rule of thumb, quilting seams are ¼ inch wide. Hand piecing allows the joining of seams with as few layers of fabric to quilt through as possible. This is because seams are only sewn as far as the next adjoining seam line. When the stitching meets the next seam line, the needle is slipped through the seam lines and the stitching is continued on the other side. This method of putting the block together gives more options when pressing seams, because none of the stitching runs into the seam allowances. This doesn't mean that the faster machine piecing is not acceptable, just be aware that there are trade-offs.

There are times when several seams meet at one point and cannot be quilted through easily. One solution is to trim the seam allowances, but if this is done, you must work more quilting in that area in order to prevent the closely trimmed seam from unraveling. Use this method only when absolutely necessary.

Or, you can use another technique I learned some time ago from a seasoned quilter: Quilt through just the top half of the sandwich, then turn the work over and quilt the same area from the back. This secures the work halfway through from the top and halfway through from the bottom.

There is a difference between pressing and ironing. When quilting, press the work. *Do not iron.* Ironing means pushing the iron back and forth on the material. This moves the threads in the fabric, distorting them, and it may push the seam lines out of shape. Pressing is the act of placing the iron directly down on the fabric and then lifting it back up without sliding the iron in either direction.

Never press seams open! Press them to one side. This eliminates strain on the seams and helps keep the batting from leaking out the seam line. It also strengthens the entire pieced block.

When possible, the seam allowance should be pressed to the darker side. This is not a hard-and-fast rule, however, and sometimes it is downright impossible to execute.

When there is going to be excess bulk in an area, press all seams in the same direction. This is also a good idea where four blocks come together. And out goes the "press to the dark side" rule.

Often there is no way to avoid several seam joints meeting at the same point. This happens when several blocks are being sewn together. Pressing the seam allowance on one block in one direction and the seam allowance of another the opposite way helps. Strive for as few layers as possible in any one spot.

Curved seams can be a challenge. Stitching carefully along the seam line is a must. Any deviation will make a difference when attaching other pieces. Allowances on curved seams should be pressed toward the convex side. It is not necessary to clip curves, which will weaken the work. Just be sure the seam allowance does not exceed one-fourth inch.

Outline quilting ¼ inch away from the seam offers the advantage of not having to quilt through four thicknesses of fabric. It also helps make the seam allowance less noticeable when it shows through light fabric.

The thin batting now available makes quilting easier, while giving quilts an antique look and feel.

The Stitches

Only two different stitches are used in all quilt making. The simple running stitch is for patchwork and decorative quilting. The slip stitch is employed in appliqué work.

The running stitch is simply weaving the needle in and out, taking short, evenly spaced stitches. The work looks like this:

– – – – – – –

Decorative quilting uses the same technique.

Appliqué is different. It utilizes tiny, invisible stitches along the seam line. After the appliquéing is completed, then the decorative quilting begins.

Quilting may be as simple or as complex as the quilter chooses. Beginning quilters tend to keep it simple, which is a good idea, as that keeps the novice from being overwhelmed. Patchwork is often quilted by outlining the patches: the quilting follows the contours of each patch in the block. By placing ¼-inch masking tape along the seam line as a guide, the quilter is able to stitch a straight, even line. The Brown Goose patch on page 30 shows this quilting pattern.

Crosshatching is another method. Evenly spaced rows are quilted in both directions, crossing each other at even intervals in an overall design. The center of the Maple Leaf design on page 50 is done in crosshatching. Here ½-inch or ¾-inch masking tape is put to good use.

For a fancier design, just mark the chosen pattern by using a purchased stencil or dressmaker carbon. If you're using the dressmaker carbon, lay it on top of the section to be marked.Put the pattern on top of this and gently trace the entire design in pencil.

If you prefer using a stencil, simply place it on top of the work. With a marker, trace the entire design.

Where the patchwork is angular, it is a good idea to use a quilting design with curved lines (as in Stormbound, page 100). This will also apply when a patchwork square is next to a plain quilted square. The overall effect will be more pleasing.

When quilting an appliqué design, shadow quilting, which follows the outline of the appliqué pieces, is a good choice. Just keep shadow quilting for several rows, with each row ¼ inch apart. After the shadow quilting starts to lose shape, the remainder of the work may be done with straight-line quilting. Crab Lou E. (page 65) uses shadow quilting.

Another method, called stitch in the ditch, has the quilting done in the seam line itself. This does not show on the top of the work but is visible on the back. It gives the same puffy effect without the stitches being conspicuous. The lighthouse and sky portions of Silent Sentinel (page 56) use this quilting method.

My quilting students always ask me about the required number of stitches per inch. My standard answer is to make your stitches as small and evenly spaced as possible. The more experienced the quilter, the smaller the stitches. In other words, don't give up what could become a satisfying hobby because your stitches aren't perfect from the start. I've seen exceptional work with stitches that were not within the 12-to-14-to-the-inch range. Color choice and care in executing the design are just as important as the length of the quilting stitches. This doesn't mean, however, that one should not strive for the tiniest stitches possible.

It is not necessary to knot the thread while piecing a block; simply backstitch at both the beginning and the end. When quilting, however, knot the thread. Draw the needle through the back of the sandwich and pull gently, bringing the knot through the backing and allowing it to lodge in the batting.

To finish off a length of thread when quilting, wrap the thread around the needle twice. Insert the needle through the top and into the batting at a slight angle. Tug the thread until the knot disappears into the middle of the sandwich. Continue bringing the needle through to the back and clip the thread.

MAKING CONTINUOUS BIAS TAPE

When it comes time to bind the quilt, making the binding can pose a slight problem. The technique described below will not only solve the problem of cutting yards of bias strips from a flat piece of material, but it will use less material than other methods.

Note: a 36-inch square will yield 13½ yards of bias tape.

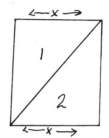

Diagram 1

Making Continuous Bias Tape

1. On the wrong side of a square of fabric (the square should be at least 18 inches), draw a diagonal line dividing the square into 2 equal triangles (see diagram 1).

2. Cut triangles apart and then stitch them back together, sewing the edges marked *X* in diagram 1 with a half-inch seam. Press seam allowance to one side, and then mark parallel lines along the bias every 1¼ inches. See diagram 2.

3. For continuous bias, fold fabric into a cylinder, bringing the sides marked Y in diagram 2 together with the right sides facing. Pin edges together, offsetting the seam by one row so that a 1¼-inch section extends at each end beyond the pinning. Match the marked lines and join in a quarter-inch seam. See diagram 3.

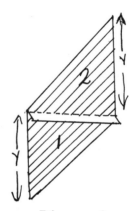

Diagram 2

4. Begin cutting along one extended marked section and continue cutting around the fabric tube as if you were peeling an apple.

5. Then press the bias strip. Fold the tape in half lengthwise with the wrong sides facing and press (don't iron!) along the entire length. Next, open the tape flat and press one side toward the center crease. After this has been done for the length of the fabric, repeat with the other side.

Voilà! You now have bias tape for finishing a quilting project. Your fingers are probably a little tender from running ahead of the iron, but the look achieved with matching bias will be worth it.

Diagram 3

APPLIQUÉ? ABSOLUTELY!

The mere mention of appliqué can send brave quilters diving for cover. Getting discouraged at the outset is what sends most of them into a tizzy. Actually appliqué is not difficult; anyone can master it with a little practice.

Appliqué is the layering of one or more fabrics on another to create a design. More complicated arrangements are no more difficult than extremely simple ones; they just take more time.

This technique is much more versatile than patchwork. Design ideas that may otherwise have to be abandoned can become a reality with appliqué. Patchwork versions of a subject are usually quite abstract, but appliqué can bring a degree of realism to any scene.

The appliqué featured in this book concentrates on slip stitching the pieces to a background material. There are many ways to appliqué, but we will cover only the slip-stitch method.

How to Appliqué

1. Place the pattern piece on the *right* side of the fabric. Draw around it with a pencil or other marker (no ballpoint pens, please). This will be the seam line.

2. Cut around the entire piece about ⅛ inch outside the seam line.

3. Fold the seam allowance toward the wrong side of the fabric. Fold under the entire edge unless some part of it will be hidden under another appliquéd piece—for example, the bottom of the cabin piece in the Red Sails in the Sunset wall hanging (page 70). There is no need to fold this under. Just have the adjoining piece (the boat hull) cover the seam and finish as usual.

4. Baste the folded pieces. Set aside. Prepare each separate piece this way.

5. After basting, the pieces need to be pressed. Don't iron—press.

6. Next, pin all the pieces in position on the background. Baste them to the background to keep them secure.

7. Sew the pieces in place with invisible slip stitches. Use a small quilting needle—nothing larger than a #10. (I prefer a #12.) A smaller needle enables the quilter to manage tiny stitches. It is also helpful to use thread the same color as the material being stitched, though I use white thread because it makes me concentrate on taking invisible stitches.

To slip stitch: Hold the work facing you in order to bring the needle through the cloth toward you. Take a tiny stitch in the background fabric. Now bring the needle up into the folded edge of the appliqué piece directly above the stitch just taken in the background, coming out about ¼ inch from the entry point. Then take another tiny stitch in the background material, directly beneath the point where the needle came out through the appliqué piece. Just continue in this manner. Remember, practice makes perfect. Can you do it? Absolutely!

Some Appliqué Tips

With your fingers, crease the background block into halves and again into fourths. This will give guidelines for placing the appliqué pieces.

Tucking ends under adjacent pieces will give the whole project a more natural look. For instance, leaves tucked under a limb will be more realistic than leaves fitted next to the limb. There's no need to baste edges that will be underneath other pieces.

The easiest way to make a circle round is to run a row of basting between the seam line and the cut edge. Cut a piece of cardboard the finished size of the circle. Place this cardboard inside the cloth circle and pull the basting thread, drawing in the edge, until it fits snugly around the cardboard. Press. Remove the cardboard and continue with the appliqué steps.

To insure sharp points on hearts, refer to the following illustration:

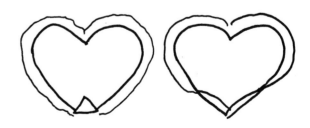

Fold up tip and press.
Next, fold in sides and press.
This will give a perfect point. Start basting. At the top indentation, clip to the seam line. Fold, press, and complete the basting. (This is one of the few instances where you press first, then baste.)

PAINLESS PILLOW PRODUCTION

Making a pillow is relatively simple. These directions, if followed carefully, will prove it.

I stuff my pillows with polyester fiberfill and blindstitch them closed. When they become soiled, I simply throw them into the washer and dryer. I do use good-quality fiberfill, and I'm sure this helps prevent lumping. It also ensures a softer pillow. By using this method, I am not limited to a specific size or shape for my pillows.

For those who prefer to use a pillow form, it is best to fashion the pillow with a zipper or other means of removing the form before laundering.

Making a Pillow

1. Make the quilt square that will be the pillow top.

2. Cut the fabric for the pillow back. This should be the same size as the pillow top.

3. Decide whether the pillow is to have a ruffle or a corded knife edge. For a pillow with a ruffle, do steps 4 through 9. When preparing a corded edge, follow steps 10 and 11.

4. To make a ruffle, prepare a length of fabric that is twice the total length of the four sides of the pillow top. For example, a 16-inch-square pillow will need a length of material that is 16 times 4 (that is, 64) times 2, for a total of 128 inches.

To determine the width of your fabric strip, double the desired finished ruffle width and add ½ inch for the seam allowance. For a 2-inch finished ruffle, you would cut the fabric 4½ inches wide.

5. Next, stitch the short ends together to make a continuous piece (see diagram 1). Fold this piece in half, wrong sides together, and press.

6. Using the longest machine stitch, run two rows of basting along the unfinished edge of the ruffle piece. Stitch one row ¼ inch and the second row ½ inch from the edge.

7. Divide the ruffle into four segments, as shown in diagram 2 (fold in half and then in half again). Pin each segment to a corner of the pillow top on the right side. Pull gathers to fit the top, adjusting the fullness so that it is evenly distributed. Pin and stitch the ruffle to the right side of the pillow top using a quarter-inch seam. This will mean the stitching is just beyond the first row of gathers. After stitching is

completed, pull out the gathering row that is ½ inch from the edge. This allows the gathers to lay evenly.

8. With right sides facing and using a quarter-inch seam allowance, pin the pillow back to the pillow front along three sides. Keeping the ruffle on the inside of this "envelope," stitch these seams. Turn right-side out and press.

9. Stuff pillow with fiberfill. (Or, if you are using a pillow form, insert zipper and stitch around all four sides.) Turn under ¼ inch on the back piece and blind-stitch the opening closed.

10. For a corded knife edge, cut a 1-inch width of fabric on the bias. Place the cable cord in the center of this bias strip and bring the raw edges together, encasing the cable cord. Using a cording (zipper) foot, stitch close to the cording. Trim the edge of the finished piece of cording so that it measures ¼ inch from the stitching to the raw edge. Place this cording along the quarter-inch seam allowance of the pillow front and pin. Stitch all around.

11. Finish the remainder of the pillow by following steps 8 and 9. Place the pillow in a place of prominence, step back, and admire it!

Diagram 1

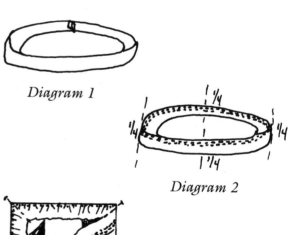

Diagram 2

Diagram 3

*Heaven Scent
—Potpourri-Filled
Coasters, page 28*

Nimble Needles—Needlebook, page 26

*Brown Goose
—Traditional Patch
Design, page 30*

PHOTOGRAPHS BY RICHARD PROCOPIO

North Star—Pillow,
page 47

A Quilter's Chatelaine,
page 40

To Wrap Our Baby Bunting In
—Carriage Robe, page 38

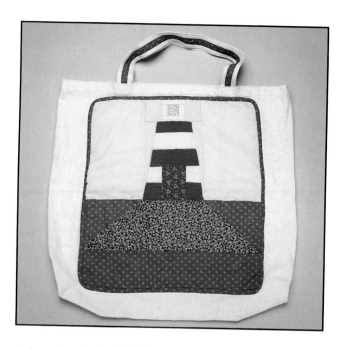

Silent Sentinel—Lighthouse Patch Design, page 56

*Mountain Seasons
—Wall Hanging,
page 53*

*Maple Leaf
—Traditional Patch Design,
page 50*

*Crab Lou E.—Casserole
Holder, page 65*

*Red Sails in the Sunset
—Wall Hanging, page 70*

Compass—Pillow, page 62

Single Tall Pine
Tree Patch

Tall Pine Tree
—Quilt, page 77

North Wind
—Pillow, page 73

Bouncing Buoys
—Bibs, Large and Small,
page 83

Snowflake Quilting Design, page 75

Lobsterboats
—Wall Hanging,
page 89

Delectable Mountains
—Wall Hanging,
page 94

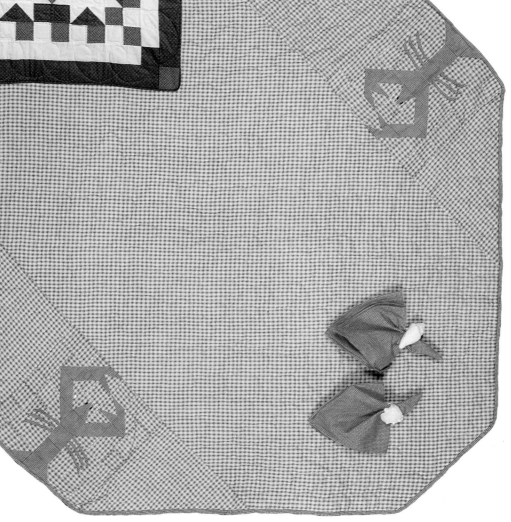

Stormbound
—Wall Hanging,
page 100

Perky Patchwork
—Picnic Set,
page 107

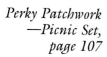

MAKE A TAG-ALONG TOTE BAG

This simple tote bag teamed with a quilted pocket is simple enough for a beginner to make, but it is also classy enough for the advanced quilter. Most of the designs described in this book would look fine on the front of this tote bag.

Why not make one for a new mother or a young scholar? It's bright and cheery for toting your favorite beach beauty's swim paraphernalia. And any knitter would certainly welcome one in the large size.

They make marvelous gifts for any occasion. And while you're stitching, don't forget to make one for yourself!

Tote bags are always handy, so gather your materials and begin sewing.

Materials

1½ yards heavy fabric such as canvas or corduroy
   for the 21-by-19-inch bag
1¼ yards fabric for the 17-by-18-inch bag

Cut

For the large bag:
One 22-by-44-inch rectangle
Two 3-by-22-inch strips for straps
For the smaller bag:
One 19-by-37-inch rectangle
Two 3-by-22-inch strips for straps

Making the Tote Bag

1. Fold the rectangle in half by bringing the short sides together with the right sides facing.

2. Tuck the folded edge up into the middle of the bag, forming the bottom of the tote. Stitch through all thicknesses. (See diagram 1.)

3. Press under ¼ inch on each long side of the two strap pieces. Bring the folded edges together and topstitch close to the edge. Now, topstitch the other long edge of the same strap. Make the second strap the same way.

4. For an extra touch, add a stripe of material down the center of each strap. Simply cut two 1-by-22-inch strips of calico. Press under ¼ inch on both long sides of these strips. Baste these to the center of the completed straps. Topstitch along the edges and *voilà!*

5. Next, carefully measuring an equal distance from each side seam, pin straps to the inside upper edge of the bag, and baste (diagram 2).

6. Make a 1-inch hem in the upper edge of the bag. Topstitch along the edge, catching in the straps as you sew. (See diagram 3.)

7. Finally, center the quilted square on the bag front and attach it by blindstitching it along three sides. You may wish to sew a snap or Velcro at the center of the pocket as a closure.

Now all that's left to do is fill the bag and start toting.

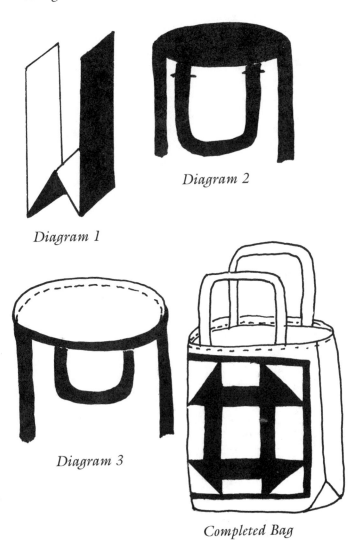

Diagram 1

Diagram 2

Diagram 3

Completed Bag

NIMBLE NEEDLES

It is a universal fact that most mothers do not know as much as their daughters. This is especially true if the mother happens to be over thirty and said daughter is thirteen or fourteen.

When our daughter Claudia was in the eighth grade, the girls were all obliged to take home economics. Claudia brought home her sewing project to finish. She just needed to complete a few details on her blouse, such as putting on the front facing, setting the sleeves, making buttonholes, and hemming.

Being the typical addlepated, middle-aged, meddling mother, I remarked that she had quite a bit to accomplish before the project could be turned in for a final grade. This notion was reinforced by the fact that she had stitched the front facings with the seams on the outside. I made mention of this and was informed that the teacher had specifically told her to sew it that way. I tried in vain to explain that the purpose of facings was to cover up raw seams but met with stubborn resistance. She finished the blouse using her own innovative methods.

Several days later, Claudia brought her report card home along with the garment. A paper attached to the blouse critiqued her workmanship. Glaring at me were the words, "facing sewn in wrong."

"I tried to tell you," I gloated.

She simply looked me square in the eye and stated that the teacher told her to do it that way and must have changed her mind. It seems the poor, over-thirty educator was as dimwitted as Claudia's mother.

There is a moral to this story. If one has the patience to wait until one's daughter is over thirty herself, then the perceived level of one's own intelligence takes a giant leap to the top. If only someone had imparted that wisdom to me years ago, it would have done wonders for my self-esteem.

Needlebooks were once a necessary item in every sewing basket. These handy items keep needles safe and sharp.

The cover of this needlebook is done in the easy Shoo Fly pattern. I've made it from black calico in honor of the infamous insect that makes gardening next to impossible in the early spring—the black fly.

Materials

22-by-6-inch piece of main color calico (MC)
Scrap of contrasting color calico for "fly" (CC)
Two pieces quilt batting 4½ inches by 4½ inches
½ yard of ⅛-inch-wide ribbon
5-by-10-inch piece of cloth for "pages." Wool is the best material because it helps keep the needles sharp.

Cut

Four #1 MC triangles
Four #2 MC squares
Four #1 CC triangles
One #2 CC square
Four 3½-by-1-inch strips of MC
Four 1-by-1-inch strips of MC
Three 4½-by-4½-inch squares of MC
Two 3¾-by-3¾-inch "pages" (wool or flannel)

Making the Shoo Fly Patch

1. Make four squares by stitching a MC triangle to a CC triangle.

2. Stitch one of these squares to each side of a MC square (see diagram 1). This is a row. Repeat this once more.

3. Stitch a MC square to each side of a CC square (diagram 2).

4. Now, sew these three rows into a patch, following diagram 3.

5. Sew a MC strip to two sides of the completed patch.

6. Stitch a CC 1-inch square to each end of the two remaining MC strips. Next, stitch these strips across opposite ends of the patch. (See diagram 4.) This completes the top block of the needle book.

7. Make a sandwich of the completed block, quilt batting, and a plain MC 4½-inch square. Baste. Make another sandwich of one plain 4½-inch square, batting, and the remaining 4½-inch square. Baste. These are the "covers" for the needle book.

8. Using ¾-inch-wide masking tape, quilt both covers using a crosshatching design. Start this by placing one edge of a piece of masking tape diagonally across the middle of the square. Now quilt along both edges of the tape. Remove the tape and place it against one row of stitching and quilt along

this. Keep moving the tape in this manner until the square is quilted in one direction. Then, place the masking tape going in the opposite direction and finish the top. It will look like diagram 5. Quilt the other cover in this same fashion.

9. Make bias binding from the MC calico by cutting 1-inch-wide strips on the bias of the fabric. You'll need 18 inches of binding for each cover. Fold in half and press. Now, bring both edges into the center and press. Stitch this around each of the quilted covers.

10. Tuck the two needle pages between the front and back covers. (You may wish to trim their edges with pinking shears.) Sew invisibly in place along one side.

11. Cut ribbon in half. Tack these to the sewn edge of the book and tie into bows.

All that's left now is to put needles inside, and the days of not knowing where to find a needle are gone. If only the black-fly problem could be solved as easily.

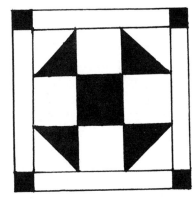

Diagram 4

Diagram 5

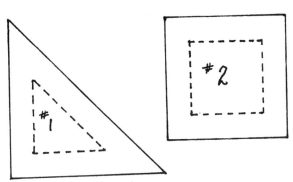

Shoo Fly Pattern Pieces

Diagram 1

Diagram 2

Diagram 3

Completed Needlebook

HEAVEN SCENT

It is amazing how scents will often trigger a memory. Once in a while when I am ironing, a whiff of that combination of dampness and heat suddenly transports me back many years to my grandmother's kitchen.

One day she was ironing in her kitchen when a thunderstorm interrupted my play. As the rain came pelting down, I ran squealing for the shelter of the cozy house, and that smell met my nostrils. Nanny was standing there with a pile of freshly pressed laundry. It was a comforting scene. Crazy as it seems, that smell makes me feel safe and secure to this day.

My grandmother passed her love of gardening on to me. There is nothing more restful than sitting in the middle of a garden and working.

During the winter when the garden is tucked in for a few months, flower smells can be recalled by setting a cup of hot liquid on one of these potpourri-filled coasters. They are extremely easy to make.

Materials for Four Coasters

22-by-6-inch piece of calico
Embroidery floss
Double-fold bias tape
Quilt batting
1 yard ribbon (optional)
Recipe of potpourri (see below)

Making the Coasters

1. Cut eight pieces of calico 4½ inches square.
2. Cut four pieces of quilt batting the same size as in step 1.

3. Transfer the shell pattern to four of the calico pieces. These will become the tops of the coasters.
4. Make a "sandwich" of one coaster top, one piece of quilt batting, and one piece of plain calico. Place a teaspoon of potpourri in the middle of this sandwich. (Separate the batting slightly and put the potpourri between the layers.)

We'll break the rules for this project: Do *not* baste the sandwich, because that will make it easier to maneuver the potpourri around during quilting. Instead, pin the layers together and quilt as usual.

5. Starting at the center, using two strands of embroidery floss, quilt along the lines of the shell pattern, shifting the potpourri around slightly as needed. Repeat steps 4 and 5 with the other three coasters.
6. Stitch bias tape around each of the coasters.
7. Stack the four coasters and tie the bundle with a ribbon.
8. A set of coasters packed with a mug and a special blend of coffee or tea makes a wonderful present for a special person in your life.

Lemon Potpourri

Mix together:
½ cup dried lemon peel
¼ cup soft cinnamon, broken into small pieces
1 tablespoon whole cloves
3 to 4 drops lemon essence

This recipe will make more than enough for the four coasters. Commercial potpourri blends may be substituted for this homemade version, and dried balsam fir needles work well, too.

Heaven Scent—*Potpourri-Filled Coasters*

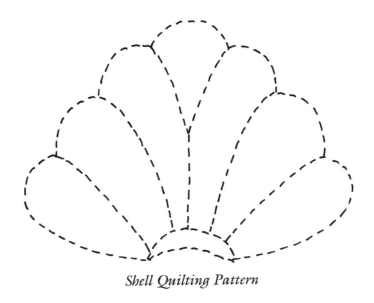

Shell Quilting Pattern

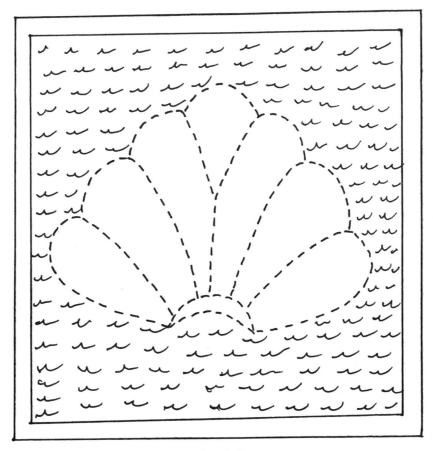

Completed Coaster

BROWN GOOSE

For fourteen years we camped at Damariscotta Lake for the summer. One year several geese spent the spring there, and one of the females laid three eggs. The geese proved to be extremely messy neighbors, and the campground owners eventually shooed them away. Our nine-year-old daughter, Andrea, decided to bring the abandoned eggs back to our campsite to hatch. (Just what I needed—to be Grandmother Goose.)

No amount of explaining would convince her that the eggs would never hatch. But after several days, Andrea realized her attempts were in vain. She traded the eggs to a friend for some other treasure. Off went her friend with the box of goose eggs.

Within two hours he was back to tell us that his mother was more than a little upset with him. It seems he had taken the eggs into their camper and left them on the table. Now, these eggs had been sitting around for heaven knows how long, and the days had been hot. Nature took its course. The eggs exploded. They were quickly whisked away, but the smell lingered for several long days.

The Brown Goose pattern dates to nineteenth-century New England and was originally done in drab colors. A modern version may combine two dark fabrics without looking dreary.

Despite its complicated appearance, Brown Goose is a very simple pattern that lends itself to any number of projects. For example, a twin-sized quilt will require seven rows of nine patches each to complete. A single patch will decorate a pillow or tote bag. Just decide on a project and turn to that chapter for the complete instructions.

Here are instructions for making the basic 15-inch patch.

Materials

¾ yard main color (MC)
¼ yard contrasting color (CC)
Quilt batting
15½-inch-square muslin

Cut

Six #1 MC triangles
Four #2 MC triangles
Six #1 CC triangles
Four #2 CC triangles

Making the Brown Goose Patch

1. Stitch one large MC triangle to each side of a large CC triangle (see diagram 1).

2. Next, stitch one small CC triangle to each side of this strip (diagram 2). Make another strip just like this one. Set aside.

3. Sew one small MC triangle to each side of a large CC triangle (see diagram 3). Repeat this step once more. Set these two strips aside.

4. There should be two large MC triangles and two large CC triangles left. Make a very large triangle by stitching one MC and one CC triangle together (diagram 4). Repeat this step with the two remaining pieces.

5. Now make a square by stitching these two large triangles together, making sure that the MC is opposite the CC color (see diagram 5).

6. Next sew one of the strips from step 3 to one end of this square. Repeat this step with the other strip from step 3 at the other end of the square. (See diagram 6.)

7. The last steps are to stitch each of the large step 2 strips to each side of the section just finished. The square is completed.

8. The only thing left to do is finish your chosen project. Refer to the appropriate chapter and continue the good work.

CC   MC

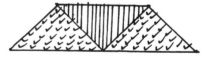

Diagram 1

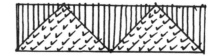

Diagram 2

Diagram 3

Diagram 4

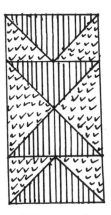

Diagram 5

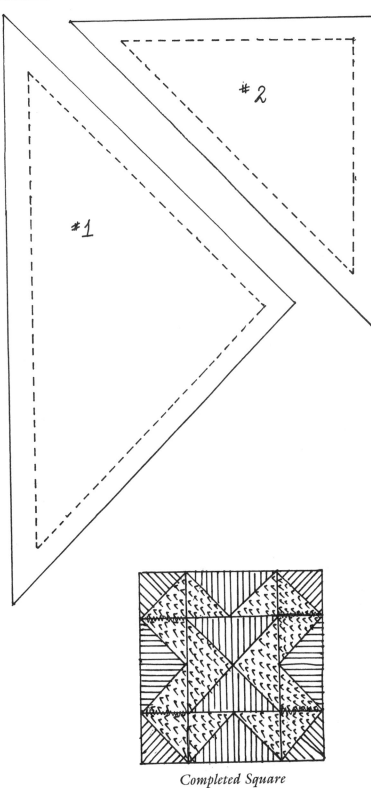

Diagram 6

Completed Square

SEASHELLS BY THE SEASHORE

We lived in Bath, Maine, for fifteen years. On the first warm Sunday each spring, we would go to Popham Beach for the first beach outing of the year. We would shiver through the picnic and visit Fort Popham, and without fail we would bemoan the fact that we did not live closer to the ocean.

We particularly enjoyed beachcombing. We dragged every piece of driftwood we found back to the car and home. We picked up beach glass, periwinkle shells, and pieces of clam shells. I especially loved the scallop shells with tiny holes in them. I thought of making jewelry with them. Some years later, I learned that whelks drilled the holes to enable them to feed on the scallops.

When we were preparing to move from Bath, we had to discard a lot of things. Determining which treasures were important enough to go with us was often a hard decision, but we still have a jar of worn glass and a variety of shells to remind us of those wonderful jaunts.

One of these springs I shall pack my sandwiches and thermos and try to rekindle some of the magic of those marvelous excursions.

Materials

Sewing pattern for your choice of skirt or jumper
Materials required for that pattern
Contrasting color (CC) material 7 inches wide and long enough to encircle the bottom of the skirt or jumper.
Four different calico prints for the shells
Batting
Embroidery thread for trimming the shells

Making the Skirt or Jumper

Following the pattern directions, assemble the skirt until it is time to stitch the last seam (preferably the center back seam). In other words, it should be one large piece that you can lay flat. This makes it relatively simple to attach the seashell band. Set this aside.

If you're making a jumper, you may or may not wish to assemble the top section at this time too.

Making the Seashell Band

1. Assemble a band of (CC) fabric 7 inches wide and the necessary length to go completely around the bottom of the skirt.

2. Determine how many shells will be needed to fit evenly along the length of this band.

3. Make templates of the shells and trace the number needed on the calico chosen for each kind. Cut out the shells, *adding a one-eighth-inch seam allowance* around each one.

4. Following the appliqué directions given on page 15, stitch the shells in place on the band.

5. Transfer the wave quilting pattern to the band. Leave about ½ inch unquilted at the top and bottom of the band; these raw edges will be finished later.

6. Cut batting to fit the seashell band. Pin the batting and band together temporarily.

7. With two strands of embroidery floss and a running stitch, outline the details on each shell. (These details are shown as broken lines on the patterns.)

8. Shadow quilt around each shell. (Keep the quilting stitches close to the shell.) Then, starting in the middle of the band and working toward one end, quilt the wave design #1. Starting at the middle once more, quilt the waves going to the other end of the band.

9. Position this band along the bottom of the skirt, with the lower edge of the band even with the bottom edge of the skirt. Pin and baste through all layers. (Baste generously to ensure that the band won't slip out of place.) Remove all pins.

10. Turn under ¼ inch along the top edge of the quilted band and slip stitch in place on the skirt.

11. With right sides together, stitch the back seam of the skirt, using a ⅝-inch seam allowance.

12. Make bias binding (see page 14) and stitch it around the bottom edge of the skirt. this eliminates the need for a hem.

13. Finish the garment according to the pattern directions.

14. Don your new attire and let the world admire your handiwork.

Periwinkle Shell

Clam Shell

Whelk Shell

Moon Shell

Scallop Shell

Completed Jumper

Piece #1
Wave Quilting Pattern

SAILING, SAILING

One of my favorite people was Ernest Maloney, of Port Clyde, Maine. My children also loved him dearly but couldn't pronounce his name. To them he was affectionately known as "Baloney."

Baloney lived to be a hundred, and was still lobstering into his seventies, which itself is no feat along the Maine coast. His claim to fame was the fact that he pulled his traps from a Friendship sloop.

One day, while he was out hauling lobster traps, Baloney started to sneeze. During one of the more powerful expulsions, his false teeth popped right out of his mouth and into the briny deep. No amount of maneuvering, even for a seasoned sailor, could retrieve them. So Baloney resorted to his lobsterman philosophy. He just announced that he "never liked the damned things anyway!"

I decided a windsock would be an appropriate token to this true Maine character—the Friendship patch is in honor of his boat, and the choice of a wind sock is inspired by his personality, which could be as gentle as a summer's breeze or as blustery as an Atlantic gale.

The Friendship pattern has been around for some time. It would also make a nifty pillow for a seafaring friend or a special quilt for a young man. For any of these projects, just use the main patch pattern and follow the directions for assembling the project of your choice.

Materials

1 yard calico for the sky
1 yard calico for the water
1 yard calico for the boat hull
(The above yardage also includes material for the tails.)
½ yard white cotton for sails and lining
8-inch macramé ring
3 yards grosgrain ribbon ⅜ inch wide
1 barrel swivel
Quilt batting

Making the Tails

1. Cut six 5-by-1-inch strips for the tails. Cut two tails from each of the three calicoes. Cut straight along the length of the material, remembering that you must cut other pieces from this same piece.

2. Fold under and press ¼ inch along both long sides of each tail. Fold under ¼ inch once more. Press and stitch. Make a hem in the bottom end of each tail, using this same method. Set tails aside.

Making the Friendship Patch and the Body of the Sock

1. Cut a length of sky calico 2½ inches by 26½ inches. Cut two 12½-by-7¾ inch pieces from the same material. Set aside.

2. Cut from sky calico
    six #1 triangles
    four #2 squares
Cut from boat-hull calico
    two #1 triangles
    two #2 squares
Cut from white cotton, for sails
    four #1 triangles
Cut from sea calico
    one 12½-by-5-inch rectangle

3. Make two squares by stitching sky triangles to boat-hull triangles. Stitch sky triangles and sail triangles together to form four more squares.

4. Following diagram 1, start to construct the sail section of the patch by stitching two sky-and-sail squares together with a sky square on either side. Repeat this row once more. Press and then sew the two rows together (diagram 1a).

5. To assemble the boat hull, stitch two hull squares together with a hull-and-sky square on either side (see diagram 2). Now sew this row to the bottom of the rows in step 4 (diagram 2a).

6. Next, add the sea rectangle to the bottom of this section (see diagram 3). This completes the actual Friendship patch.

7. Stitch one of the 12½-by-7¾-inch pieces of sky calico to the the left side of the completed patch. Repeat with the other sky piece on the right side. Press seam to one side.

8. Now, sew the 2½-by-26½-inch narrow strip to the top of this. Press carefully.

The Quilting

1. Cut a piece of quilt batting and a piece of plain cotton the same size as the completed top. Sandwich the top, batting, and plain cotton piece together and baste.

2. Following the quilting diagram, and using wave quilting design, quilt through all layers.

Assembling the Windsock

1. Using a flat-felled seam, stitch the short ends of the quilted patch together, forming a cylinder. (To make a flat-felled seam, simply stitch a regular seam with the raw edges on the outside of the project. Trim one side of the seam to ¼ inch. Turn under the raw edge of the widest part and pull it over the short side. Stitch, being sure the entire seam lies flat.)

2. Press under ¼ inch at top of sock. Fold down an additional 1¼ inches and press toward the inside of the sock. Place the macramé ring under this fold and stitch the seam closed.

3. Cut the ribbon into three 1-yard lengths. Pin and stitch one end of each ribbon to the top of the windsock, spacing them evenly around the circumference of the ring.

4. Thread the lengths of ribbon through the barrel swivel. Bring the loose ends of the ribbon down to the ring and tack them to the top of the wind sock, matching them up with the ends already attached to the sock.

Attaching the Tails

1. Fold under ¼ inch around the bottom edge of the windsock body, and press. Fold under 1¼ inch again. Press and baste.

2. Fold under ¼ inch (toward the right side of the fabric) along the top of each tail. Place this end up under the bottom edge of the sock top. Pin in place, keeping the hem and the folded-down end of the tail even. Repeat with the rest of the tails, alternating colors.

3. Stitch through all layers.

Your windsock is ready to hang. Place it where everyone can enjoy looking at it.

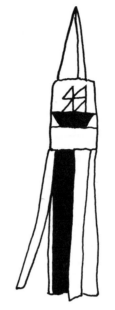

Completed Windsock

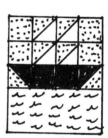

Diagram 1

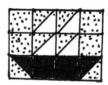

Diagram 2

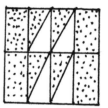

Diagram 1a

Diagram 2a

Diagram 3

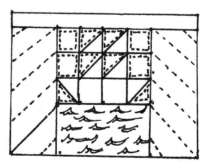

Quilting Diagram

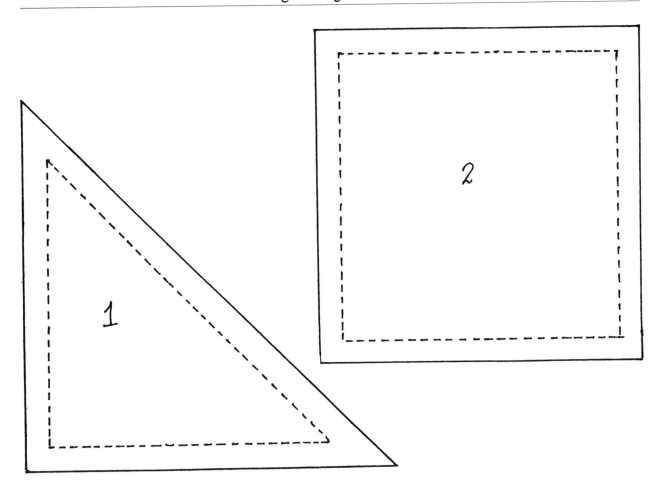

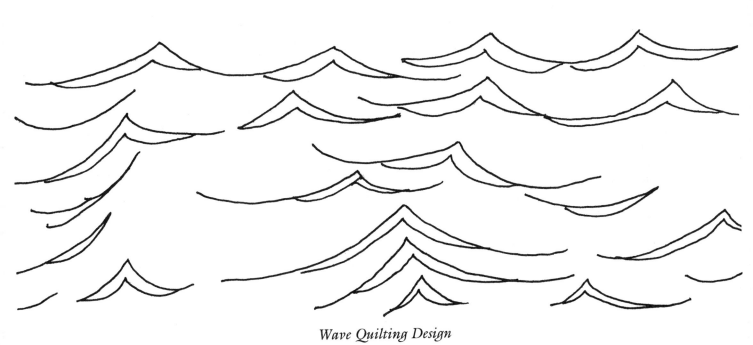

Wave Quilting Design

TO WRAP OUR BABY BUNTING IN

I found that having four children in four and a half years was not too bad. I didn't think too much about cleaning hands, tying shoes, or washing diapers, because it was part of my daily routine. When we traveled somewhere as a family, the kids just lined up to have their coats buttoned, their hats adjusted, or whatever else needed doing. Life became quite methodical.

But there was one incident I will never forget. Our son Michael was about a month old, and we were preparing to go away for the day. I got together the diapers, extra clothing, and the other paraphernalia required when traveling with small children, and my husband packed the car. The kids were sent outside with Dad. When it was finally time for me to don my coat, I walked out, closed and locked the door behind me, and got into the car.

We just sat there for a few minutes. Finally, I asked Gary why we weren't leaving. He stared at me for several seconds and then very seriously asked if I didn't think it would be a good idea to bring the baby.

I had carefully dressed Michael for the trip, wrapped him in his blanket, and left him lying on the couch.

After that I always counted noses.

When the Clamshell design originated in Colonial New England, it was totally utilitarian and made up of dark wools. Made with bright modern fabrics, it assumes a lively beauty.

What child wouldn't love these colorful patches? Though the pattern is Clamshell, I'm certain that most little folks will see them as bright, bouncy balloons.

Scraps are the order of the day with this design. However, even scrap quilts need a degree of planning. The example shown in this book was made with soft, subtle colors using a variety of prints. The important thing to remember in a scrap endeavor is to make the prints and colors blend inconspicuously. One part should never be too pronounced.

This pattern lends itself to any size project. It can be made larger or smaller just by adding clams to the length and/or width.

Materials

Child's carriage robe (or small crib quilt) is approximately 33 by 42 inches.
   Scraps, scraps, scraps
   1 yard muslin
   1½ yards calico for quilt backing and binding
   Quilt batting

Cut

Approximately 170 clamshells

Making the Clamshell Quilt

Note: The big secret to the successful execution of this design is careful cutting, marking, and basting at each step.

1. Make a template using the clamshell pattern. Place this template on the straight of the fabric and cut around the outside.

2. Cut approximately 170 clamshells, then trim the seam allowance from the template and place it back on each clam. Trace around the altered template on the right side of the fabric. This clearly marks the seam allowance.

3. Fold the convex (top) seam allowance toward the wrong side of the material. Press and baste. Leave the concave seam allowances lying flat. Set aside the shells after basting each one.

4. Press the muslin backing. Lay it on a flat surface. In order to keep the clams aligned evenly, they will be basted to the muslin.

5. Starting from the top of the muslin, pin the first shell to the backing, leaving a quarter-inch seam allowance at the top. Pin a second shell next to the first one with the lower sides touching. (See the shell diagram.) Continue pinning the remainder of the first row this way.

6. To cover the muslin where it shows in the spaces along the tops of the first row of shells, simply tuck pieces of fabric between the shells. Baste these pieces and the first row of clams at this time.

7. The second and subsequent rows will be done by basting a clam between the concave lower sides of the two shells in the row above it, covering the seam allowances as you go. Each row will either start or

end with a half clam. Just keep adding rows until the top is the desired size.

8. After the correct number of rows have been basted to the backing, the last row will be trimmed straight across the bottom, leaving only the top half of the clamshells.

9. Permanently attach the clamshells to the muslin by slip stitching along the top of each one.

10. Trim the edges of the quilt top even with the muslin all around. Remove all basting.

11. Make a sandwich of the top, the batting, and the calico backing. Baste securely.

12. Quilt the entire top ¼ inch inside the contour of each shell, or, using 2-inch-wide masking tape, quilt in a crosshatch design.

13. Trim off the excess batting and backing.

14. Make bias binding from calico and stitch it around the quilt.

Now all you need is a little one to wrap in this comfortable quilt. And as my children used to say, the baby will be able to "snuggle bunny" any time.

Completed Square

Placing the Shells

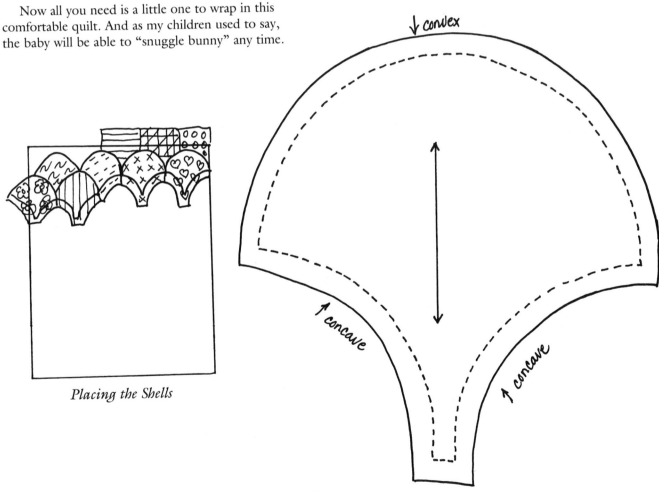

Clamshell Pattern

A QUILTER'S CHATELAINE

The chatelaine (pronounced *shat' 'l an*) dates back to medieval France, when the lady of the house carried one for holding keys, needles, thread, or whatever she might need that day. These "little pockets" were an essential part of her daily apparel.

Our youngest daughter, Andrea, was a champion frog-catcher from the age of four. She often earned her mad money by selling them for bait. Of course, it cost me more for laundry detergent to clean her clothes after a frogging excursion than she earned, but how could I discourage this budding entrepreneur?

We were eating dinner one evening when Andrea reached into her pocket and produced a small frog. She sat patting it as the other kids raised a ruckus about having a frog at the table. In fact, they had quite a lot to say about frogs in general. I was trying to maintain my composure at the sight of my pigtailed tomboy looking puzzled at all the commotion. It was, after all, just a frog.

Her older brothers and sisters would not let up, and suddenly, in one final nervous gesture, Andrea started to put her thumb in her mouth for comfort and stuck the frog in my mistake.

The older kids squealed. Andrea fought back tears. My husband, having endured the disruption long enough, commanded her to put the frog down immediately. She did, and in one giant leap it landed square in the middle of my husband's dinner.

This little pocket will do more than hold frogs. The quilted front is a pincushion. The back has a pocket for thimble and thread. The attached tape measure, with a small pair of scissors dangling from the end, can be looped around the quilter's neck. Everything for a day of quilting is close at hand. These directions tell how to make a chatelaine with a corded edge, but a narrow ruffle or bias binding also work well for finishing the edges. You really should make a chatelaine; it is a handy addition to any sewing basket.

Materials

4-by-4-inch square of plain color
Small scraps for corners
12-inch square for front strips, back, and pocket
3-by-3-inch piece for heart
5½-by-5½-inch square of batting
5½-by-5½-inch piece of muslin
24 inches of cording, either purchased or custom made (see page 16, steps 10 and 11)
Fiberfill
6-inch piece of ¼-inch wide elastic
Tape measure (preferably cloth)
Grosgrain ribbon 64 inches long, ¾ inch to 1 inch wide
¾-inch-wide masking tape
Small pair scissors

Preparing the Pieces

1. Make templates for each pattern piece.
2. Cut one #1 and four #2 pattern pieces from chosen fabric. Remember to trace the heart on the right side of the fabric and to add a seam allowance as you cut.
3. From the 12-inch square of fabric, cut a 5½-by-5½-inch square for the back, a 4¾-by-5½-inch piece for the pocket, and four #3 rectangles.

Making the Quilted Square

1. Sew two #3 rectangles to opposite sides of the plain 4-by-4-inch center square.
2. Sew a #2 square to each short end of the two remaining #3 rectangles.
3. Pin these rectangles to the other two sides of the center square. Stitch. Press.
4. Fold under and press the seams of the heart. (See page 15 for directions on preparing the heart.)
5. After the heart is ready, place it on the center of the plain square. Measure at several points to assure correct placement. Pin, baste, and slip stitch the heart to the square.
6. Prepare a sandwich of the muslin, the batting, and the top square with the heart. Baste.
7. Quilt with a crosshatching pattern using the ¾-inch masking tape as a guide. After completing the quilting, set aside.

Making the Pocket

1. Fold down ¼ inch on one long edge of the 4¾-by-5½-inch pocket piece. Press. Turn under another

¼ inch and stitch across, forming a casing. Run the elastic through this casing and fasten securely at each end.

2. Run a gathering thread along the bottom edge of the pocket.

3. With the wrong side of the pocket facing the right side of the back square, pin and baste the pocket to the sides of the back. Pull the gathering thread to fit the bottom of the back square, adjusting the gathers evenly and baste. Set aside.

Assembling the Pincushion/Pocket

1. Baste the cording trim to the front edges of the pincushion.

2. Place the quilted front and the back together with right sides facing. Stitch around three sides. Turn right-side out and press. Stuff with fiberfill. Still leaving one side open, continue with the next step.

Preparing the Tape Measure

1. Place the tape measure on the grosgrain ribbon. (The ribbon should extend one inch beyond the "60-inch" end of the measuring tape and 3 inches beyond the "1-inch" end of the tape.) Stitch along both sides of the tape as close to the edge as possible. Don't trim the extra ribbon.

Note: To help hold the tape in place as you stitch, run a glue stick along the back of the tape before placing it on the ribbon.

2. Fold in the raw edge of the pincushion pillow. Slide the extra grosgrain ribbon at the "60-inch" end of the measuring tape into the opening at the left corner, and slip stitch in place.

3. At the other end of the tape, fold under the raw edge of the grosgrain ribbon and hem. Slip this ribbon through the finger opening of the scissors, bring the ribbon back on itself to form a loop, and either slip stitch it together or sew on a snap fastener or Velcro so the scissors can be easily removed.

Completed Square

Add ⅛-inch seam allowance when cutting

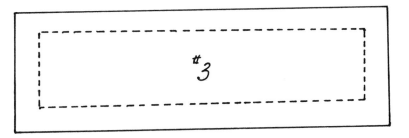

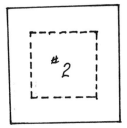

THE VILLAGE GREEN

Many towns have small parks or village greens where townsfolk gather for special occasions or just to sit and enjoy life. The high school band often performs at these special events. Village greens make me think of high school bands—and an embarassing episode from my days as a high school musician.

I played the sousaphone when I was in high school, and on one occasion our band played a combined concert with another area school. We performed in their auditorium, which was undergoing renovations.

The curtain opened and the members of the bands filed onto the stage and climbed the makeshift bleachers set up on a five-foot-high temporary stage. Two sousaphones were perched way up on the top step. I nervously climbed the steps and reached to pick up my huge horn. Not realizing the bell of the other horn overlapped mine, I picked up one instrument and sent the other brass goliath crashing to the floor twelve feet below.

I would have gladly welcomed the floor opening up to swallow me. The young man who played the other tuba could have easily pushed me after his horn.

These place mats, with their center square surrounded by smaller squares, symbolize the town park's relationship with other parts of the town and its activities.

The triangles at each end signify the fact that, although we may head in different directions, still we are partly influenced by whatever touches us as we journey through life. Perhaps we're all small-town people at heart.

Materials

These place mats are oversized: 15 inches by 20½ inches finished dimensions.

- Many different fabrics of the same basic color. (I used ten. The varied prints and shades of the same color look good together because there are quite a few of them. Often, two or three shades of the same color don't blend well, but when a few more shades are added, they merge into a pleasing combination.) Scraps will be enough for most of the pieces.

- The backing will require about 1¼ yards of calico for backing. (This will also give enough extra material for the two rectangular strips at the top and bottom of the mat.)
- Batting

Cut for Each Place Mat

One #1 square
Twelve #2 squares
Two #3 triangles
Four #4 triangles
Two #5 rectangular strips

Making the Place Mats

1. Arrange the #2 squares around the large #1 square. Stitch two #2 squares together and sew to the side of the #1 square. Repeat this on the other end of the #1 square. (See diagram 1.)

2. Make two rows, each consisting of four #2 squares. Stitch these rows to the remaining sides of the #1 square. This makes a large center square. (See diagram 2.)

3. Stitch a #4 triangle to each short side of a #3 triangle, forming a rectangle (diagram 3). Repeat this once more.

4. Stitch one of these rectangles to opposite ends of the large center square (diagram 4).

5. Sew a #5 strip to each long side of the place mat (see diagram 5). Press.

6. Mark the heart quilting designs on the top following diagram 6.

7. Cut backing at least ¾ inch larger all around than the completed top patch. Cut batting allowing a little extra around the outside.

8. Baste the top, the batting, and the backing together in a sandwich.

9. Quilt the place mat, starting with the hearts in the center. To quilt around the small squares and triangles, use ¼-inch masking tape as a guide.

10. Trim batting even with the top. Next, trim the backing to ½ inch wider than the top. Now, bring the backing toward the front to form the binding. Turn under ¼ inch of this binding and press. Slip stitch the binding in place, mitering the corners.

One place mat is finished. Following these same steps, complete the set. Cook your favorite meal, invite a few friends in, and show off these new mats to your heart's delight.

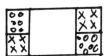

Diagram 1

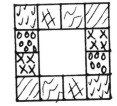

Diagram 2

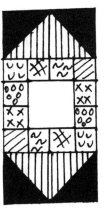

Diagram 3

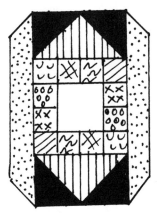

Diagram 4

Diagram 5

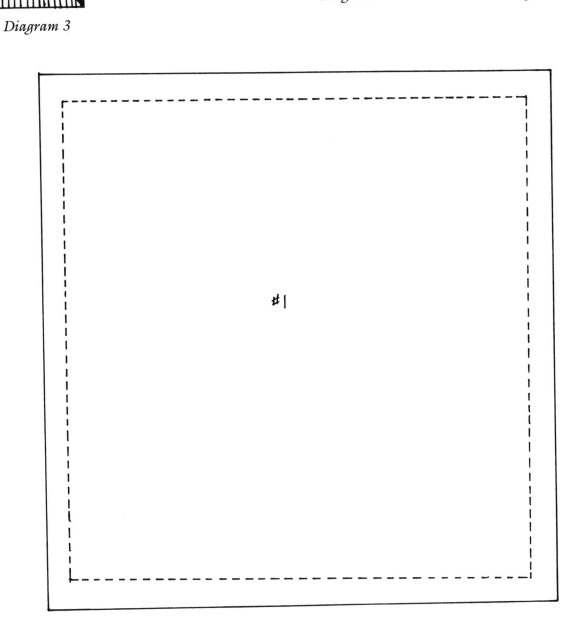

#1

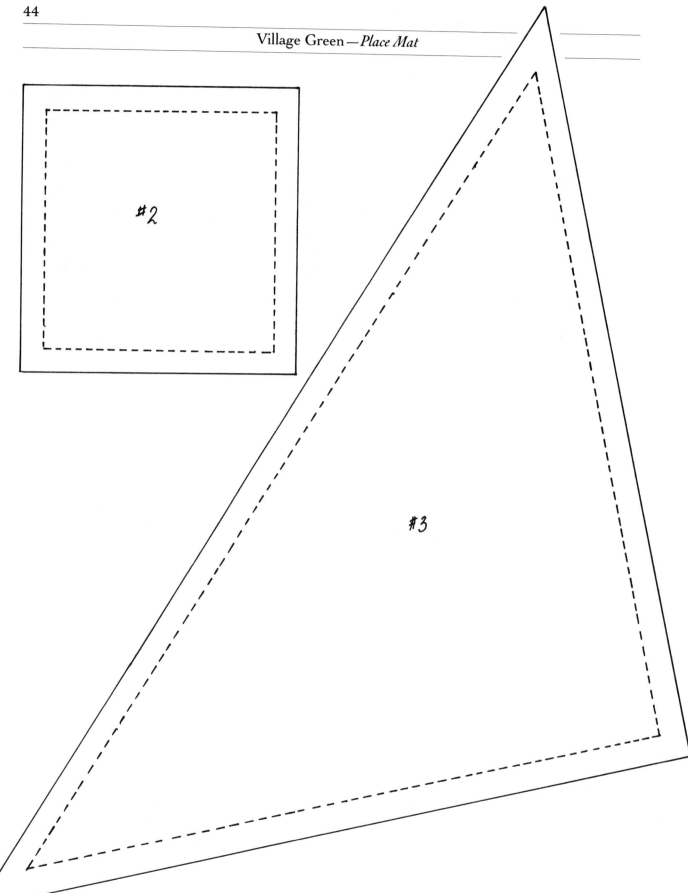

#2

#3

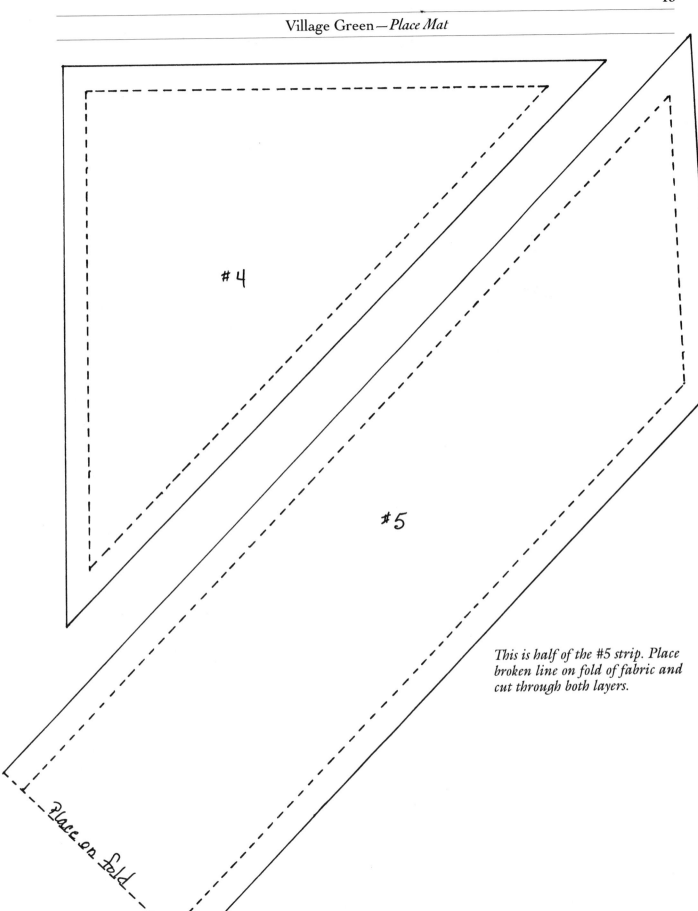

#4

#5

This is half of the #5 strip. Place
broken line on fold of fabric and
cut through both layers.

Place on fold

Diagram 6

*Quilting Design
for Center Square*

*Quilting Design for the
End Rectangles*

NORTH STAR

When I pause to admire the night sky, filled with twinkling constellations, memory transports me back to my first camp out as a young Girl Scout, when I learned how to find the North Star. Years later, my friend Judy and I became official Junior Girl Scout leaders, for a year. Things went fairly well as long as we each supervised the other's daughter.

The last hurrah for the year was a weekend camp-out with other area troops. Not too long before, a Scout had disappeared from a camp out somewhere in the West, but Judy and I tried not to think about that. We concentrated on maintaining our sense of humor and keeping our nerves in check.

After the campfire on the last evening, as the girls were preparing for bed, ten-year-old Kelly suddenly came running from the outhouse, screaming hysterically.

Fearing the worst, Judy and I tried to console her and count heads at the same time. Finally, after much cajoling, the truth emerged. Our Scout was using the facilities at the same time as another troop leader. When the leader stood up, she accidentally knocked Kelly's flashlight into the hole.

Our young miss was screaming because her mother was "going to kill" her! This mother was my friend and neighbor and a very good parent. She had, however, told her daughter that the newly purchased flashlight had better not be lost.

Our sense of relief sent Judy and me into gales of laughter. The overwrought girl did not appreciate our amusement and was rather perturbed that scout leaders would laugh at such a grim situation.

It is said that some good comes from every tragedy. In this case, we enjoyed a well lit outhouse. Between the flashlight and the glow from the bright, starry sky, no one had any trouble finding her way to the latrine for the rest of the night.

The North Star design, with its small, curved pieces, is not for the novice, but it will satisfy the more advanced quilter who is looking for a challenge. It is tricky, especially around the center, but the result is more than worth the effort of piecing it together.

This pattern would make a great gift for a special occasion, although with all the work involved, you just might choose to keep it for yourself. (Mine is living at my house.) Make a pillow, a tote bag pocket, the center square for a sampler quilt, or be really brave and do a complete quilt.

Materials for a 13-by-13-inch Pillow

⅝ yard main color (MC)
½ yard contrasting color for borders, center, and cording (BCC)
¼ yard contrasting color for star points (SCC)
Scrap for small semicircles
13½-by-13½-inch piece of muslin for patch backing
Batting
1⅝ yards cable cord
¼-inch-wide bias tape

Cut

Note: Part of the secret to success with a difficult pattern is exercising great care when cutting out the pattern pieces.

Four #2 MC pieces. Cut these on the bias.
Four #5 MC triangles
Four #6 MC pieces
One 13½-by-13½-inch MC square for pillow back
One #1 BCC center
Four 16½-by-2-inch strips BCC
1⅝ yards bias strip BCC for cording
Eight #4 SCC star points. When cutting these, cut four with the pattern facing up and then turn the pattern face down and cut four more.
Eight #3 semi-circles from scrap. Cut these on the bias.

Making the North Star Patch

1. Lay out the entire patch on a flat surface. Keep putting the pieces back in place as they are stitched. (It might be wise to piece this patch by hand, since hand piecing affords more flexibility when stitching small, intricate pieces.)

2. Stitch the four #2 pieces around the #1 center (diagram 1). When piecing convex curves to concave curves, start by finding the center of each piece. Match the centers and corners. Pin. Stitch. There is no need to clip curves.

3. Next, add the eight #3 semicircles around this

center section (diagram 2). Set aside.

4. Sew one #4, a #5, and another #4 together. Stitch a #6 piece to one side of this segment. (See diagram 3.) Repeat this three more times.

5. Now, carefully stitch these sections to the center section.

6. Finally, finish the four seams connecting the star sections.

7. Sew a border strip to the top and one to the bottom of the patch. Then sew the remaining two strips to the remaining two sides, mitering the corners.

8. Make a sandwich of the muslin backing, the batting, and the patched top. Baste.

9. Quilt ¼ inch around each pattern piece using the masking tape as a guide.

10. If you are using the patch for a pillow, finish it according to the directions in "Painless Pillow Production" (page 16).

Completed Square

Diagram 1

Diagram 2

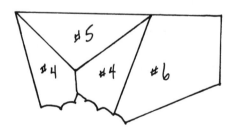

Diagram 3

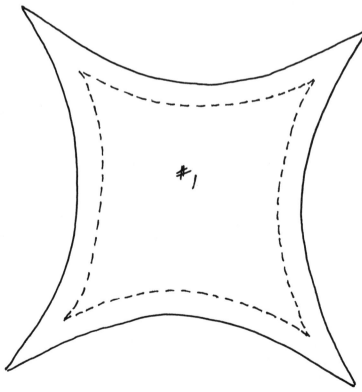

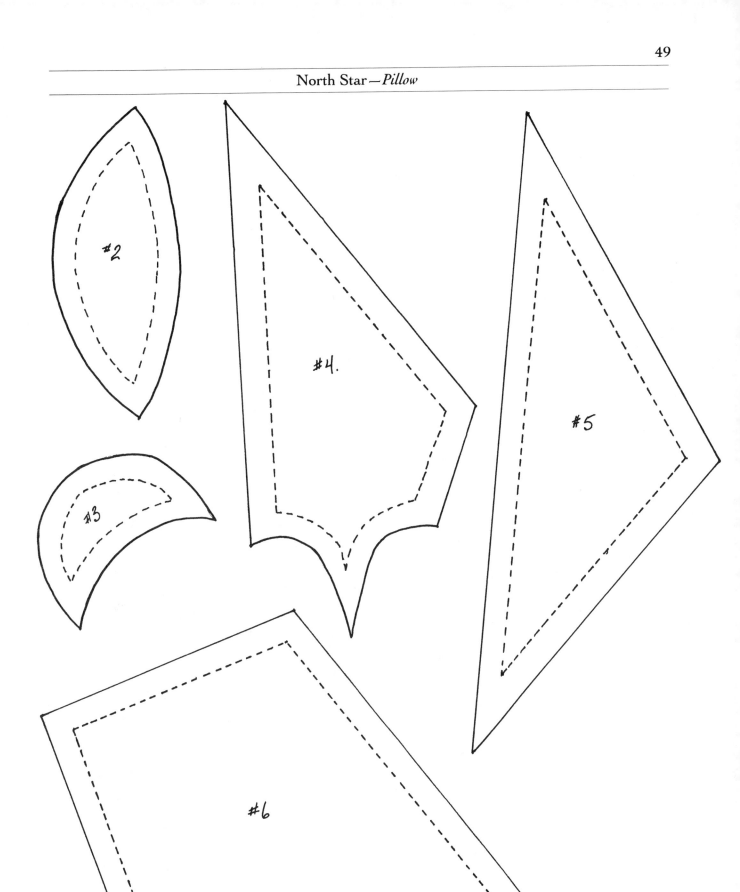

MAPLE LEAF

One year our older girls chose wildflowers as their 4-H project. The leader's children had made the same choice. One warm day, the leader called and invited us to go wildflowering with her family. Armed with our best books on identifying these ornaments of nature, we set out.

I still remember the beauty we found along one logging road. A small stream danced among the rocks. The trees were only partially leafed out, and the sun shone brightly through their sparse tops.

We found lots of spring flowers, and the kids picked and pressed a specimen of each variety.

At midday, we sat on rocks and logs to enjoy our lunch in those tranquil surroundings. The warm sun and the peace of that spot encompassed our entire group. I silently pledged to return again soon, but of course, we never did go back.

I still love to roam through the woods, and I have a particular affinity for the trees and flowers in our area.

As with the familiar wildflowers, most people can readily identify the maple leaf. Maples, of course, are also appreciated for their spectacular range of fall colors. For the quilter who is a purist, this allows some leeway when choosing fabric for the traditional Maple Leaf pattern, which hails from the early 1800s. This particular variant of the Maple Leaf design, while it looks more complex than some, is actually one of the easier ones to piece together. (That's one of the great things about quilting; the pattern is not always as complicated as it looks.)

A small tote bag with the Maple Leaf square stitched to the front will carry treasures for anyone. It will even keep a stash of wildflowers safe.

Materials
The actual patch is 8½ inches square. With borders it measures 12½ inches square.
¾ yard background color (BC) calico
⅛ yard light contrasting color (CC) calico
⅛ yard dark main color (MC) calico
Batting

Cut
One 13-by-13-inch BC square for backing
One #1 BC square

Four 8½-by-8½-inch BC border strips
Three #2 BC rectangles
Three #4 BC squares
Eight #3 BC triangles
One #1 MC square
Three #4 MC squares
Eight #3 MC triangles
One #6 MC stem
Four #2 CC rectangles
Four #5 CC squares

Making the Maple Leaf Square
1. Lay out the patch on a flat surface.
2. Stitch together one #3 MC triangle and one #3 BC triangle to make a square. Make eight of these.
3. Stitch two of these squares together four times, following diagram 1.
4. Now, sew one of these rectangles to a #2 CC rectangle, forming a square (diagram 2). Repeat this three more times.
5. Next, stitch a #4 MC square to a #4 BC square (diagram 3). Repeat this twice more.
6. Stitch a #2 BC rectangle to each of the rectangles just finished in step 5, making three squares (diagram 4).
There should now be a total of nine squares, including the one #1 BC square and the one #1 MC square. Since Maple Leaf is a nine patch, the next step is to make three rows.
7. Start sewing the squares together as in diagram 5, forming three rows. Now sew these rows together.
8. The #6 stem should now be appliquéd to the lower right-hand BC square. Place it according to diagram 6. At this point, the actual Maple Leaf patch is done and it is time to add the border.
9. Stitch a BC strip to each side of the patch.
10. Sew a CC #5 square to each end of the remaining two BC strips. Sew these to the top and bottom of the Maple Leaf patch.
11. Make a sandwich of the BC backing, the batting, and the completed top. Baste.
12. Quilt the entire square, following the quilting diagram.
13. With scissors, trim the square evenly all around.

14. Make BC seam binding (see page 14) and sew it around the trimmed square.

15. If you've chosen to use this square as the pocket for a small tote bag, now is the time to stitch it securely to the front of the bag, then start gathering treasures.

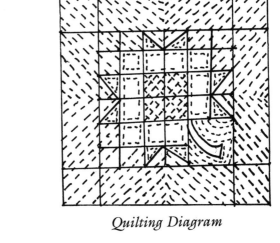

Quilting Diagram

Diagram 1 *Diagram 2* *Diagram 3*

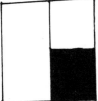

Diagram 4

☐ ■ ▨
BC MC CC

Diagram 5

Diagram 6

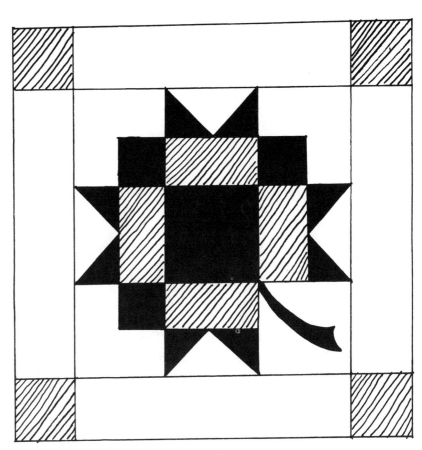

Completed Square

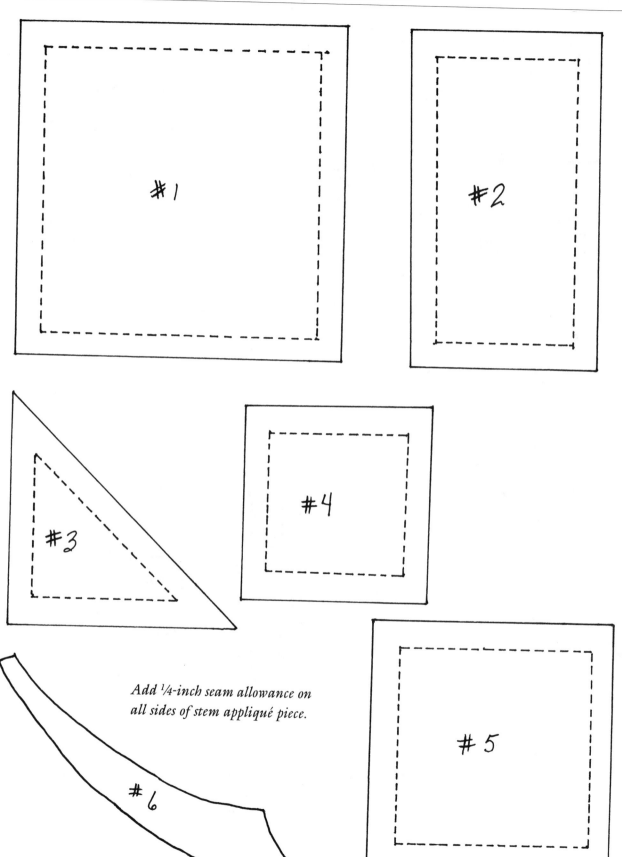

#1

#2

#3

#4

#5

Add ¼-inch seam allowance on all sides of stem appliqué piece.

#6

MOUNTAIN SEASONS

As a young girl, I thought I could never love anything the way I love the ocean. It still holds a large and special spot in my life, but nine years ago my fickle heart found a new attraction. It is not a replacement but a fresh and exciting infatuation.

My new love is Megunticook Mountain. Even when I'm not looking at the mountain, I'm conscious of its presence. I am smitten by the constant changes of its raiment.

In the summer Megunticook is attired completely in shades of green. Rain and fog give the green a somber tone. The sun casts shadows and the clouds make patterns on its slopes.

Fall is my favorite time of the year, and Megunticook seems to reflect my mood by coming alive with the variegated hues of autumn. My heart sings as I tuck my garden in for the winter.

Early winter finds me bundling in my warmest clothing and withdrawing to the fireside, while the mountain stands naked against the gray skies. My view is better then, and I pause more often to gaze at its stark beauty.

Winter gradually gives way to new life. Spring rejuvenates the mountain with a crisp, fresh cover, and my whole being is also revitalized. As the sun warms the earth, it invigorates my body, and I am ready for the world.

When life is not going smoothly, rock solid and steady Meginticook reminds me that, no matter what happens, there is a stable and constant base to level things, and everything will eventually be fine.

Perhaps, you say, maturity alone would have brought me ultimately to this serene philosophy. My stalwart friend and I know better.

Each of the blocks in this wall hanging represents a season. The center square depicts water—lake or ocean. The four triangles surrounding this square symbolize mountains, while the pieces fitting between the mountains signify the seasonal skies. The large corner triangles suggest the universe as well as tying the other blocks together.

This is another versatile design that may be used in a variety of ways. The individual blocks can be made into pillows or pockets for tote bags. More squares may be added to make any size quilt. For a table cover, just add borders around the outside to produce the desired size. Finally, you can stitch bone rings along the top back of the design and use as a small wall hanging, as described below.

Materials

The overall size of the wall hanging is 26 inches square. The individual season squares are 12 inches square.

Scraps for the water, mountain, and skies
½ yard for large corner triangles
1½ yards for backing, lattice strips, and bias binding
Batting

Cut

Sixteen #1 triangles
Four #2 triangles for each season (16 total)
Eight #3 triangles for each season (32 total)
Sixteen #4 triangles
Two 12½-by-2½-inch lattice strips
One 26½-by-2½-inch lattice strips
27-inch square for backing
27-inch square batting
1-inch-wide bias strip about 106 inches long (see page 14 for instructions on how to make a continuous bias strip)

Making the Season Blocks

1. Each season block is made up of four smaller squares. Start by stitching the short sides of two #3 triangles to two sides of a #2 triangle (diagram 1).

2. Next, referring to diagram 2, sew a #1 triangle to the third side of each #2 triangle.

3. To the top of that composite triangle, sew a large #4 triangle (diagram 3) to form a square.

4. Construct three more squares in this manner.

5. Now, matching points, stitch one of these squares to another. Stitch the other two squares together also.

6. Finally, stitch these two sections together to form the final block (diagram 4).

7. For the wall hanging, make three more blocks exactly like the first one—just change the season colors for each.

8. Attach a short lattice strip to one side of a season block. Sew another season block to the other side of the lattice strip (diagram 5).

9. Repeat step 8 with the other two season blocks.

10. Now, stitch a seasons section to each side of the long lattice strip (diagram 6). Press the whole thing.

11. Make a sandwich of the backing, the batting, and the completed top. Baste.

12. Quilt the entire top, starting with the lattice strips. Quilt the season blocks using 1-inch-wide masking tape and starting at the inner corner and working toward the outer edge. Quilt each block individually and the final design will form a somewhat continuous pattern that represents the seasons going around and around. (See quilting diagram.)

13. Stitch bias binding around the entire outside of the hanging.

14. Attach small rings, evenly spaced, to the back of the hanging along one side (this will be the top). Have the top of the rings even with the top of the quilted hanging. This allows it to hang evenly against the wall without the rings being conspicuous.

There! If you are not fortunate enough to have the real mountain, you can enjoy the changing seasons just by looking at this lovely bit of handwork.

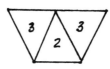
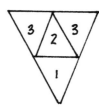

Diagram 1

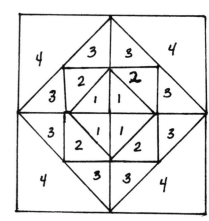

Diagram 4

Diagram 2

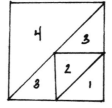

Diagram 3

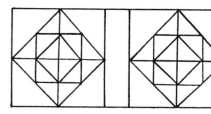

Diagram 5

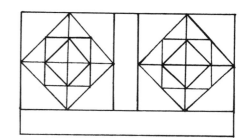

Diagram 6

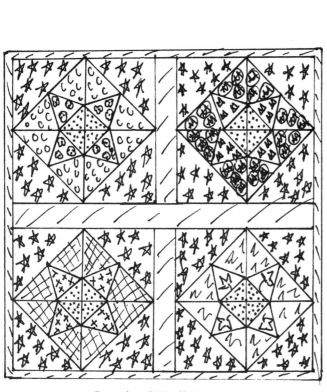

Completed Wall Hanging

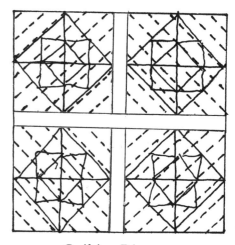

Quilting Diagram

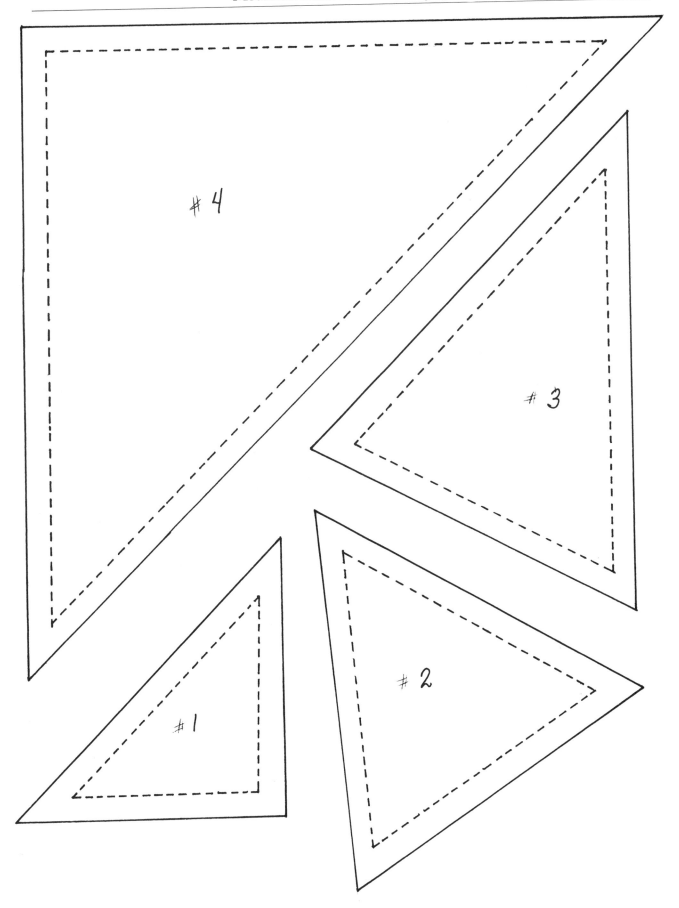

SILENT SENTINEL

The lighthouses and Coast Guard lifeboat stations that used to dot the rocky coastline were protective sentinels to the men who earned their living from the sea. Now all the lighthouses have been automated, and the lifeboat stations have long since been closed.

My Uncle Wes was in the lighthouse service, and I spent many childhood days visiting with my cousins at Newagen Light. I vaguely recall hunting, cooking, and eating periwinkles on one of these visits. A poor man's *escargot*, you might say.

Another of my relatives, Uncle Lew, was retired from the Coast Guard. One afternoon, our family went for a visit to Burnt Island lifeboat station, where he had once been assigned.

Now, both my dad and uncle were overgrown imps and always full of mischief. So it came as no surprise to this eleven-year-old when my father, accompanied by my cocker spaniel, Scruffy, wandered into the woods in search of a billy goat Uncle Lew had told him was living there.

He was gone for some time, when suddenly the quiet was interrupted by shouting and barking.

I ran to the window and saw my father being chased by the goat, while the dog nipped at the animal's feet. Every so often the goat lowered its head to butt Scruffy.

I remember crying uncontrollably at the sight of all this commotion. My father came flying through the door just as the goat was about to imprint him with its horns. Seeing my distress, my dad scooped me up, hugged me tight, and began teasing me for worrying about him.

As soon as I calmed down, I informed him I hadn't been worried about him; I was crying because I thought the goat was going to kill my dog.

This patchwork lighthouse square fits nicely on the front of the large tote bag described on page 25. The bag will carry all the gear one needs for a day's outing on land or sea.

Materials

The completed patch is approximately 15 inches by 16 inches.

⅜ yard calico for sky
¼ yard calico for rocks
1 yard calico for sea, block back, and strap trim
Scraps of muslin and red calico for lighthouse stripes
Scrap calico for door
Scrap for light
Batting

Cut

The pattern pieces are numbered according to their place in the design.

One 17-by-18-inch piece of calico for patch backing
One #1 sea rectangle
One #2 rocks piece
Two #3 sea triangles—cut one, turn pattern face down, and cut one
Two #4 red stripes—cut one, turn pattern face down, and cut one
One #7 red stripe
One #9 red stripe
Two #5 muslin stripes—cut one, turn pattern face down, and cut one
One #8 muslin stripe
Two #11 muslin pieces
Two #13 muslin pieces
One #6 door
One #12 light
Two #10 sky pieces—cut one, turn pattern face down, and cut one
Two #14 small sky rectangles

Making the Silent Sentinel Patch

1. Lay out the entire patch on a flat surface. After stitching, return each piece to its proper position in the patch.

2. Stitch the two #3 sea triangles to the two short sides of the #2 rocks, forming a rectangle (see diagram 1).

3. Pin the long #1 sea rectangle to the bottom of the rectangle just completed (diagram 2). Stitch. Set aside.

4. Next, piece together the entire lighthouse following diagram 3. Start by stitching one #4 red piece to a #5 muslin piece. Repeat this with the other #4 and #5 pieces, making sure that you end up with a left-hand pair and a right-hand pair. Sew these pieces to each side of the #6 door, as shown in the lower portion of diagram 3.

5. Now stitch the #7 red stripe to the top of the

section just finished. Follow this with the #8 muslin stripe attached to the top of that. Complete this section of the lighthouse by adding the last #9 red stripe to the top.

6. Finally, stitch the two #10 triangles to the sides of this part. This completes the "tower" of the lighthouse (diagram 3). Set aside.

7. For the "light" section, start by adding the #11 muslin pieces to each side of the #12 square. Then add the #13 muslin pieces to the top and bottom of this. To complete this section, stitch a #14 small sky piece to each side. (See diagram 4.)

To finish the lighthouse section, pin and stitch the completed light square to the top of the lighthouse patch stitched in step 4 (see diagram 5).

8. Finally, pin and stitch the lighthouse section to the sea section. Press the entire square.

9. Make a sandwich with the backing square, the batting, and the completed patch. Baste.

10. Quilt the patch. Stitch in the ditch around the sky and lighthouse sections. Transfer the wave quilting pattern #2 to the sea portion of the patch and quilt. Allow some of the sea quilting to "splash" onto the rocks.

11. Trim the batting even with the top patch.

12. Next, trim the backing to ½ inch wider than the top.

13. Bring the backing forward to form a binding. Turn under ¼ inch of this binding and press. Slip stitch the binding in place, mitering the corners.

14. If using this patch on a tote bag, center the patch on the front of the bag and slip stitch sides and bottom securely in place. Add a fastener to the top, if desired.

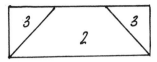

Diagram 1

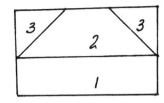

Diagram 2

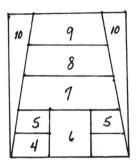

Diagram 3

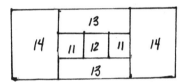

Diagram 4

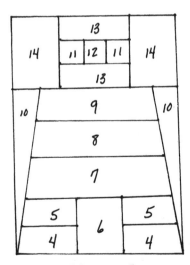

Diagram 5

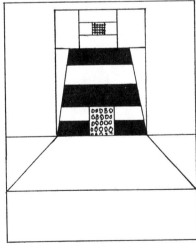

Completed Wall Hanging

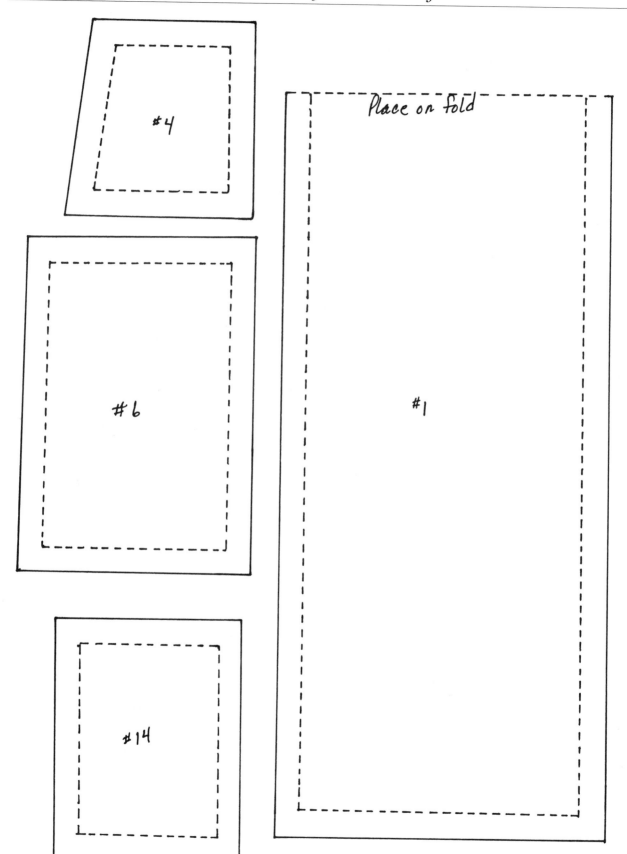

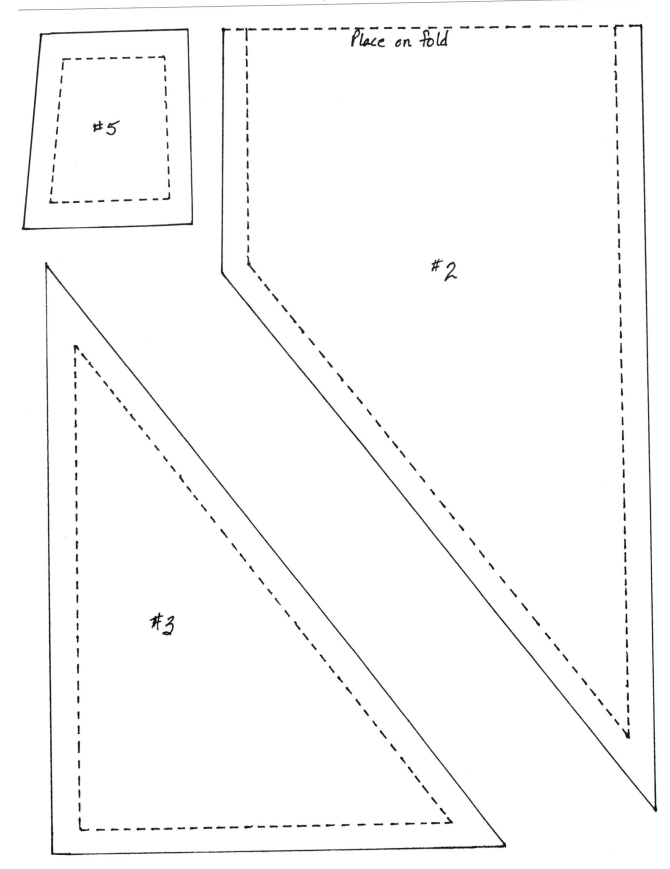

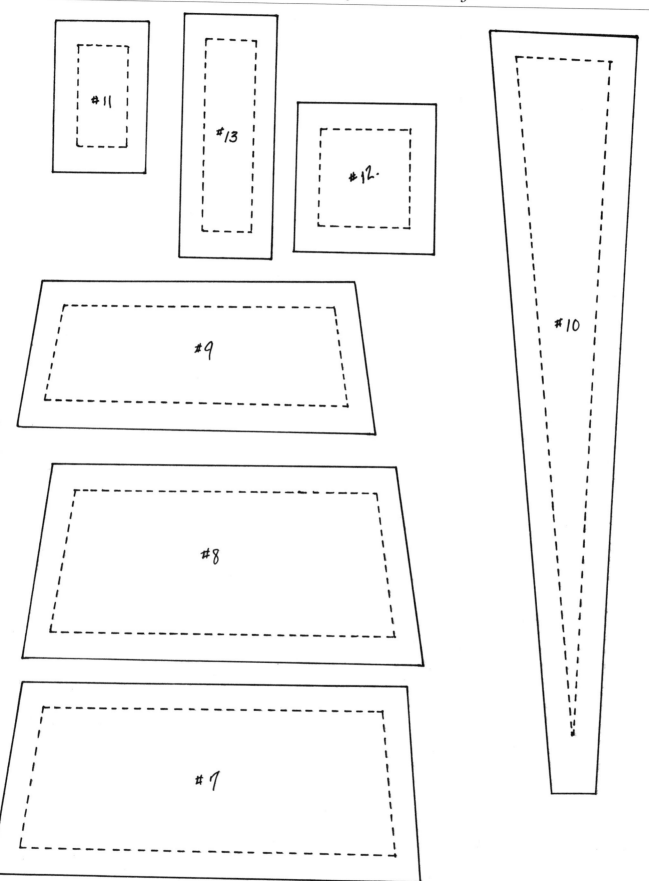

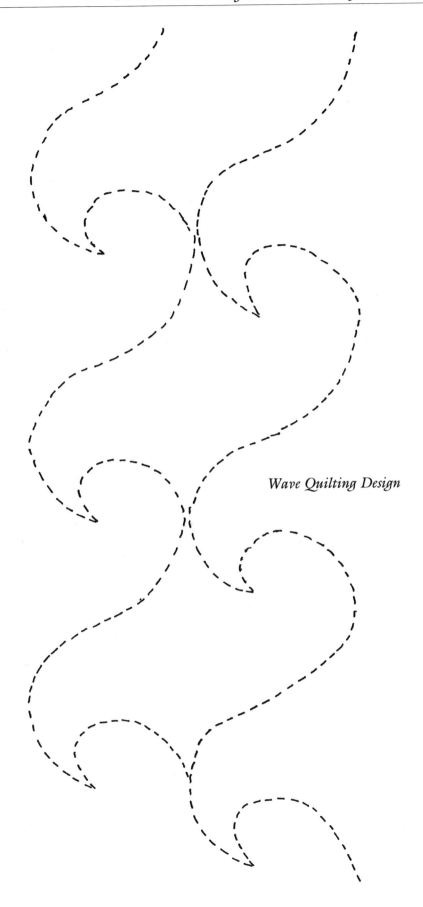

Wave Quilting Design

COMPASS

Anyone who ventures onto the ocean or into unfamiliar territory needs a compass. It is imperative to know where you are along the fog-shrouded coast. It is also necessary to take your bearings when the only thing in sight is open ocean.

My mother delighted in relating the story about the time when as a new bride she went with my father to haul his lobster traps. He announced that she could navigate the boat while he busied himself with other tasks.

She asked him what course to follow, and he replied she only needed to head for "that island over there." Well, she looked and looked but could see nothing but sky and water. So she inquired once more.

Now, my dad was a mild-mannered man, but he was quickly becoming perturbed. "I told you to head for that island over there. Just point her in that direction and quit asking questions."

My mother did as she was told, and about fifteen minutes later "that island" loomed large on the horizon.

She remained puzzled about this until the day she died. She never knew whether his instincts or a sneak peek at the compass had given him his powers of direction. And a close-mouthed lobsterman would never reveal his secrets.

This beautiful geometric design is not for the beginner. The pattern dates from around 1930 and should be done in a combination of two colors, one dark and one light.

The following instructions assume that you are making a pillow from one patch, but, should you feel ambitious, several Compass patches joined together make a spectacular quilt.

Materials

Makes a 17-inch-square pillow with corded edge.
¾ yard contrasting color (CC) light (also used for pillow back)
½ yard main color (MC) dark
17-inch-square muslin
Batting
Fiberfill
Cable cord

Cut

Sixteen #1 MC triangles
Sixteen #1 CC triangles
Eight #2 MC pieces
Eight #2 CC pieces
Eight #3 MC pieces
Eight #3 CC pieces

Making the Compass Patch

1. The patch is made up of sixteen small squares. Each square consists of two #1 pattern pieces, one #2 piece, and one #3 piece. Sort the cut pieces into 16 sets. There will be eight sets with MC #2 triangles, and CC #1 and #3 pieces. There will also be eight piles with opposite colors, i.e., CC #2 triangles with MC #1 and #3 pieces.

2. Stitch a MC #1 pattern piece to each side of a CC #2 piece (see diagram 1).

3. Now, stitch the curved side of a CC pattern piece #3 to the curved part of the section just finished (diagram 2). Press. Make seven more small squares exactly like this. Set aside.

4. Next, assemble the eight small squares, that have the colors reversed.

5. Lay out the whole block as it will look when finished. As you work, pick up only the squares to be stitched together at each step and replace them after stitching. this will ensure that you keep all the pieces in their correct places.

6. Make a row of four squares, following diagram 3 for color placement. Repeat this one more time.

7. Then make a row of four squares following diagram 4. Repeat this once more.

8. Finally, stitch the rows to each other to complete the patch.

9. Make a sandwich of the Compass patch, batting, and the muslin square. Baste.

10. Quilt the entire block. This pattern is effective when stitched in the ditch.

11. Make cording using MC. (See page 16, steps 10 and 11 for cording instructions.) Baste the cording to the front of the quilted block, having the raw edges even.

12. Finish constructing the pillow by following the instructions for pillow making in "Painless Pillow Production," page 16.

MC *CC* *Diagram 1* *Diagram 2*

Diagram 3

Diagram 4

Completed Patch

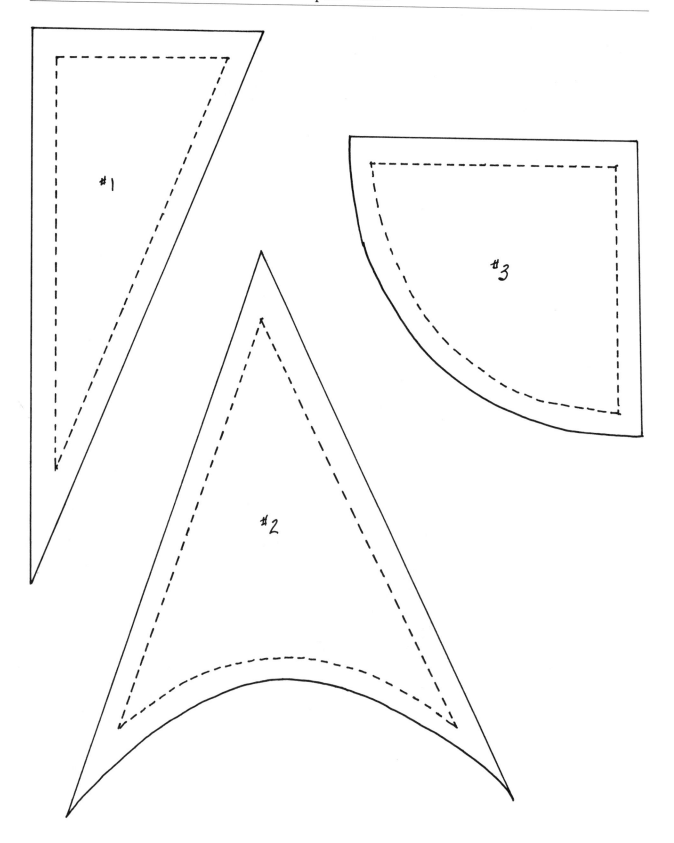

CRAB LOU E.

This nifty casserole holder will allow you to remove a hot dish from the oven without burning your hands. Prepare the following recipe for Crab Lou E. and serve it for dinner. Be sure to use your new casserole holder to take it from the oven.

Recipe for Crab Lou E.

5 tablespoons butter or margarine
4 tablespoons flour
2½ cups milk
10 ounces sharp Cheddar cheese
1 teaspoon Worcestershire sauce
½ to 1 teaspoon salt
Dash of pepper
4 ounces crabmeat
1¼ cups frozen peas, cooked
1 tablespoon dried parsley flakes
1 slice dry bread

Melt 4 tablespoons of butter. Stir in the flour. Slowly add the milk, stirring constantly. Add the cheese, which has been grated or cut into chunks. Cook slowly until mixture is thickened.

Add the Worcestershire sauce, the salt, and the pepper. After the sauce is thick, stir in the crabmeat and the cooked peas. Add the parsley flakes. Pour into individual baking dishes or a shallow dish such as a quiche pan.

Put the bread in a blender and make crumbs. Melt the remaining 1 tablespoon of butter. Add the crumbs and toss together. Sprinkle these over the top of the crabmeat dish(es). Bake at 350° for 20 minutes or until browned.

Serve over toast. Team with a fresh green salad. Enjoy!

Materials

¾ yard main color (MC)
¼ yard contrasting color (CC)
Batting
¾-inch-wide masking tape

Cut

Two MC holders (refer to step 5)
MC bias strip, approximately 88 inches long
Two MC mitts (one for left hand and one for right hand)
Two CC mitts (one left and one right)
Two CC complete crabs
One holder from batting
Four mitts from batting

Making the Casserole Holder

1. Make templates for each crab part and trace them onto CC material. Cut out the parts, adding a one-eighth-inch seam allowance all around each piece.

2. Following the appliqué directions in the "Appliqué? Absolutely!" chapter (page 15), baste the crabs in place on the MC mitts. Position them so one of the front claws is on the thumb of the mitt. Blind-stitch around each crab. Embroider eyes and antennae.

3. Make a sandwich of a CC mitt, batting, and an appliquéd mitt. Baste. Repeat with the other mitt.

4. Quilt each mitt. With the masking tape as a guide, quilt crosshatching on the crab body. Then quilt closely around the crab body and legs. Next, shadow quilt around the outline of the entire crab to the edges of the mitt. Set aside.

5. Tape the short sides of two pieces of newspaper together. Fold in half along this taped seam. Place pattern piece #1 on this newspaper, with the dotted line of the pattern along the fold line of the newspaper. Trace around the other three sides. Unfold the newspaper.

Next, place the #2 mitt pattern at one end of this tracing, matching notches, and trace around it. Finally, move the #2 mitt pattern to the other end of the traced #1 piece, matching notches, and trace around it once again. The result should look like the holder diagram. Place the newspaper pattern on the MC fabric and cut two MC holders with mitts.

6. Make another sandwich of one MC holder, batting (use one complete holder batting and add another mitt batting on each end), and top it with the other MC holder.

7. Either by hand or with a sewing machine, crosshatch-quilt the entire holder.

8. Stitch bias binding across the top wrist of each crab-decorated mitt. Pin mitts to holder, matching hands.

9. Stitch bias binding around the entire holder, securing the mitts to the backing. Make a small clip where the thumb and hand meet.

Crap Appliqué Pattern

Crab Lou E. — *Casserole Holder*

Completed Casserole Holder

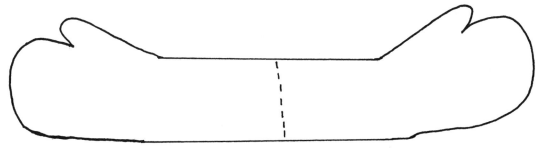

Holder Diagram

Place on fold

Center Section of Holder

#1

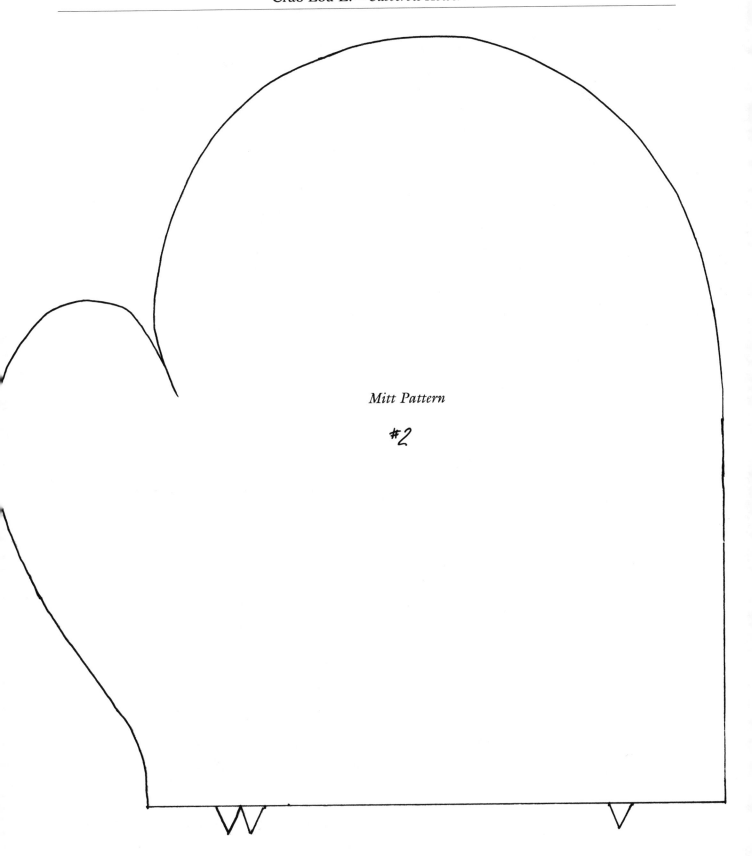

Mitt Pattern

#2

RED SAILS IN THE SUNSET

The back yard of my childhood home had a ledge at the top of a small incline. I vividly remember looking out the window one evening just at sunset and seeing my father silhouetted against the blazing fall sky. His large frame was black against the tangerine backdrop. The trees stood stiff and pointed as he walked toward the house. The whole scene was indelibly imprinted on my mind.

Many years later, on the sixth anniversary of my mother's passing, my dad lay close to death. My heart was heavy that September evening as I went to the window and looked toward the harbor.

The scene before me brought a rush of nostalgic wonder. There in the dusk was the same autumn sky with black trees silhouetted against it. I was spellbound and filled with melancholy.

But, at the same time, a peace came over me, and I knew in my heart that my father's suffering needed to end. I said a silent adieu to him at that moment, but I have never had to say goodbye, because I carry enough of him inside me to sustain me for the rest of my days.

This small hanging (or large pillow) is reminiscent of windjammer sails set against a twilight sky as the vessel heads for a safe harbor.

Whenever you see a beautiful sunset, stop and enjoy. It is one of life's perks.

Materials

1 yard MC for ocean, backing, and bias binding
¼ yard CC for sunset sky
Scraps for boat hull, cabin, two sails, flag
10½ inches bias tape for mast
Batting

Cut

The overall square is 18 inches by 18 inches
One MC backing 18½ inches by 18½ inches
One MC ocean piece 12½ inches by 18½ inches
One CC sky 6½ inches by 18½ inches
One #1 boat hull
One #2 cabin
One #3 sail
One #4 sail
One #5 flag

Making the Red Sails Square

1. Stitch the sky rectangle to the ocean piece, forming the background square.

2. Make a template for each of the five appliqué pieces. Trace these pieces onto the intended fabric and cut out, being sure to add a one-eighth-inch seam allowance all around.

3. Following the appliqué directions in the "Appliqué? Absolutely!" chapter (page 15), position the five sailboat pieces on the background square as shown on the completed patch diagram. Don't forget the bias-tape mast.

4. Make a sandwich of the backing, the batting, and the completed sailboat square. Baste.

5. Quilt around the sailboat, sails, mast, and flag, stitching close to the appliquéd pieces. Transfer the wave quilting pattern from the Seashells project (page 34) to the ocean part of the square and quilt along these lines.

6. Make bias tape and sew it around the square with small, invisible stitches.

7. Add small rings to the back of the completed square for hanging.

Completed Wall Hanging

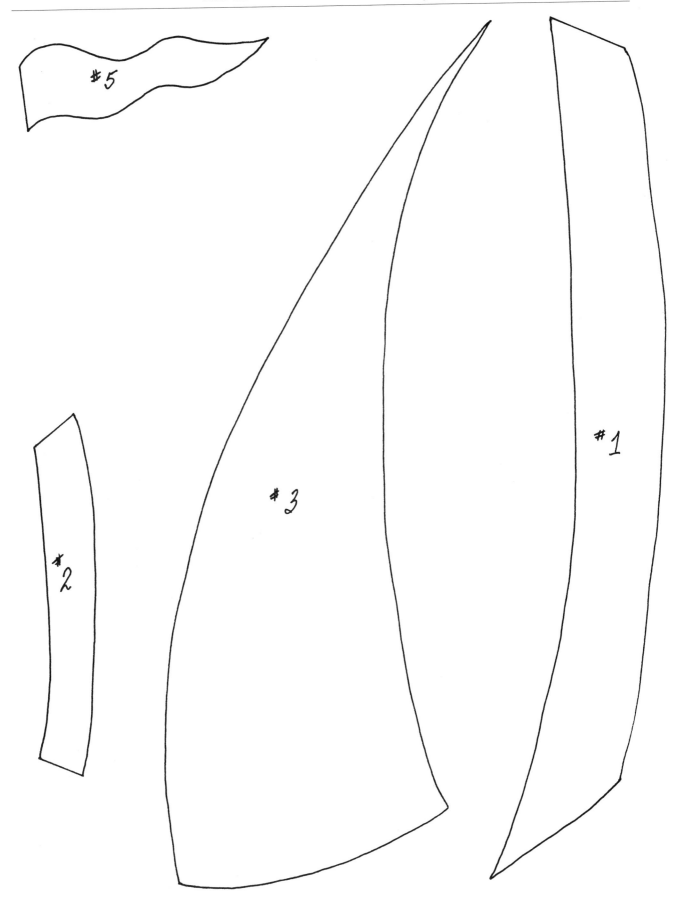

#5

#1

#3

#2

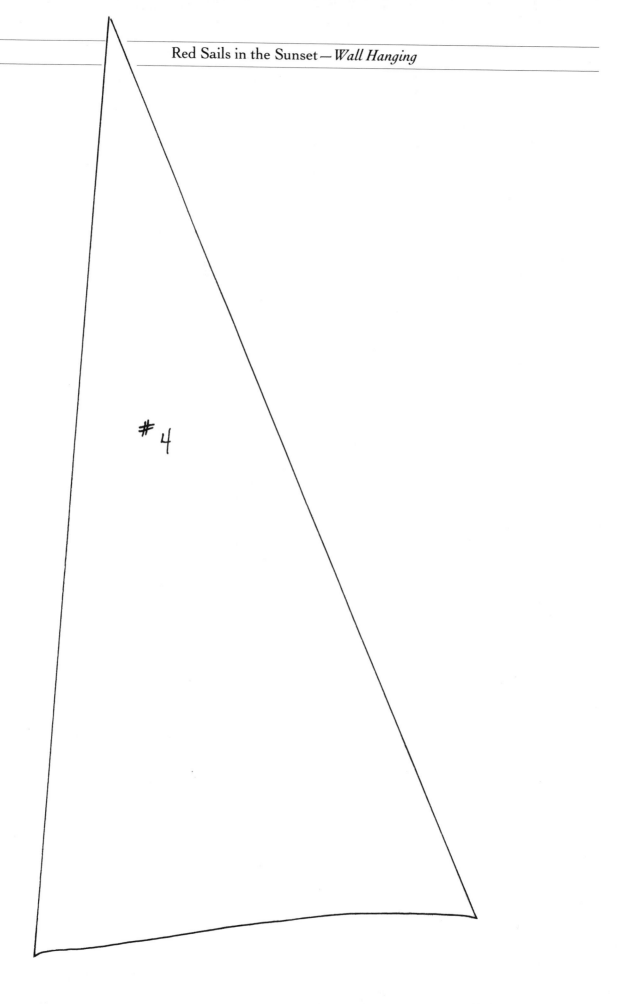

#4

NORTH WIND

My friend Sylvia related a wonderful story to me. One of the American hostages held in Iran, Richard Queen, was being released for health reasons after eight and a half tense months. He'd be staying with his parents, who lived in a nearby town. Sylvia and the proprietor of a local store decided to have a welcoming quilt made for him

Sylvia organized the project, the store donated the materials, and women on the nearby island of Islesboro made the quilt. Many hands gathered together in goodwill for a mutual goal.

The quilt was fashioned with a pine tree center motif decorated with fifty-two yellow bows—one for each of the Iran hostages. Surrounding the tree were pieced friendship squares, with four appliquéd corner squares depicting Maine scenes.

My friend presented the quilt to Mr. Queen on a bitterly cold December day. She was impressed with his warmth and friendliness. He, in turn, loved the quilt and appreciated the gesture.

Quilts do more than warm our bodies; they have a way of warming our souls as well. When the north wind blows this winter, we'll give thanks for our lives and remember those who are less fortunate.

This is an excellent undertaking to pursue when the winter wind is howling outside and you are tucked indoors where it is toasty and warm. As with many of the other patterns in this book, this one lends itself well to larger projects, if you wish to make something larger than the ruffled pillow described below.

Materials

For a 12-inch-square pillow with ruffle:
 ¾ yard main color (MC)
 ¼ yard contrasting color (CC)
 12-by-12-inch square of muslin
 Batting
 ¼-inch-wide masking tape

Cut

 One 12-by-12-inch MC square for pillow back
 Two MC strips for ruffle, 5 inches wide by width-of-fabric
 One #1 MC triangle

 Five #2 MC triangles
 One #1 CC triangle
 Five #2 CC triangles

Making the North Wind Patch

1. Lay out the patch on a flat surface.
2. Stitch three #2 MC triangles alternately with two #2 CC triangles, referring to diagram 1.
3. Now, stitch the large #3 MC triangle to the short side of the row made in step 2 (see diagram 2).
4. Next, make the other half of the patch by sewing three #2 CC triangles alternately with two MC triangles as in diagram 3.
5. Then, add the large #1 CC triangle to the short side of this row, following diagram 4.
6. Finally, finish the patch by sewing together the two larger triangles made in steps 3 and 5, taking care to match the points of the triangles (diagram 5).
7. Make a sandwich of the muslin square, batting, and the North Wind patch. Baste.
8. Quilt around all triangles, using the masking tape as a guide.
9. Complete the pillow by following the pillow-making instructions in the "Painless Pillow Production" chapter (page 16).

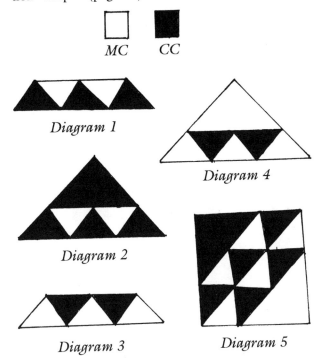

MC CC

Diagram 1

Diagram 2

Diagram 3

Diagram 4

Diagram 5

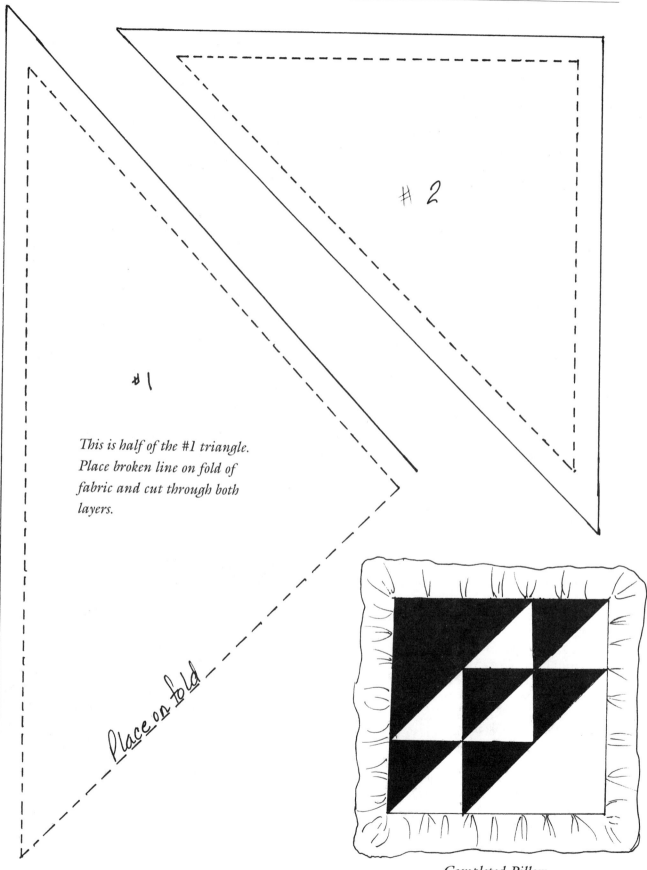

2

#1

This is half of the #1 triangle.
Place broken line on fold of
fabric and cut through both
layers.

Place on fold

Completed Pillow

SNOWFLAKE

Old-timers swear that snows of yesteryear were much more severe than the storms of the present. Of course, the old-timers of previous generations were also spouting the same notion.

As a young girl, I remember an eighty-year-old gentleman relating stories about "no'theastas that started in December and hardly let up until April."

No'theastas? That's right, no'theasta. It is not "nor'easter," as most dictionaries on how to talk Maine would lead one to believe. The word is "no'theasta." Just ask anyone whose livelihood has come from the waters of coastal Maine—ask a true Mainiac.

Mainiac, now there's a word. I first heard it when I was in high school. I think the summer kids invented that term. And believe me, we native teenagers did not like it one bit. We relished that word about as much as we native girls enjoyed seeing those cute summer females arriving every June and turning the heads of all the boys in town.

Those girls were *soooo* tan. They were golden when they arrived. We could never figure out how they managed it, since their school year extended later into June than ours. I now suspect that the last weeks of study were actually a newfangled course called Bronzing 101.

We local girls stood no chance at all. We really didn't have time to lie toasting in the sun. After all, we were too busy cleaning up after the season's last wild snowstorm.

This design is done with white quilting thread on a white square or with white thread on a colored background. (I made the sample with light blue thread only so it would photograph better for this book.) It can be used as a single project or can easily be incorporated into a larger article such as a wall hanging or a quilt. Team the Snowflake pattern with one of the patchwork designs, and the result will be quite lovely.

Materials

Square of white cotton, size optional. (The sample is 14½ inches square.)
½ yard calico for the back
Square of muslin the same size as the white cotton
Quilt batting
Dressmaker's carbon (optional)
For a pillow, as shown in photo:
Cable cord (for a corded pillow)
Fiberfill or a pillow form

Transferring the Design

1. Transfer the Snowflake design to the white cotton using one of the following methods.

Method A: Using a quilt marker, trace the design directly onto the cloth. Often with white or muslin material it is possible to use the cloth like tracing paper and simply lay it on top of the design to be copied.

Method B: Use dressmaker's carbon. Center the carbon on top of the cotton square. Trace the snowflake pattern from the book. Center and pin the Snowflake pattern on top of the carbon. With a pencil, lightly trace the entire design, being careful not to press too hard but with enough pressure so that the design comes through onto the cloth.

2. Make a sandwich of the muslin, the quilt batting, and the cotton square. Baste the three layers together.

3. Quilt the entire design using white thread. Remember to always start from the center and quilt toward the outer edges.

4. Last but not least, finish the square into your chosen project, referring to the chapter that covers that method.

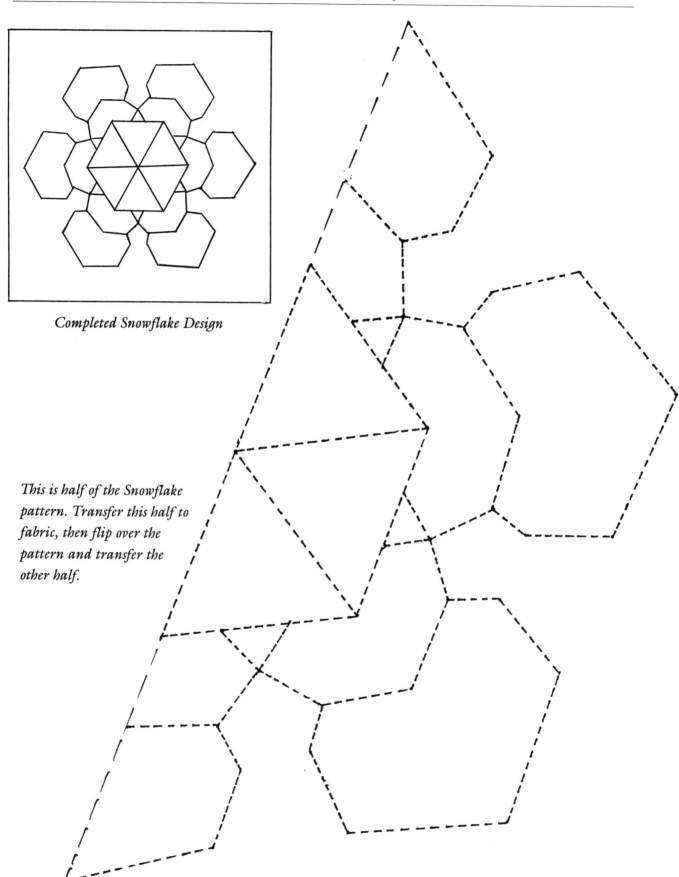

Completed Snowflake Design

This is half of the Snowflake pattern. Transfer this half to fabric, then flip over the pattern and transfer the other half.

TALL PINE TREE

If you have never seen a chipmunk scurrying around looking for food or mischief, or perhaps both, you have missed one of life's delights.

Chipmunks are curious, and when they have been around humans for a while, they will become somewhat tame. They love to eat, especially humans' food. Friends of ours once told us about a camping trip where the only thing their resident chipmunk would eat was chocolate doughnuts.

One afternoon found the campground kids with nothing to do. Then one of the older boys appeared with a fishing rod with a large peanut tied to the line in place of a fish hook. He sat in a lawn chair at the edge of the woods and cast the line. As he slowly reeled in the peanut, a curious little head appeared. Soon the mischievous chipmunk was hooked—not with a fish hook, mind you, but with the fun of bouncing along after that moving morsel.

The game went on for some time, until the kids tired of it. They decided to let the little rodent have his treat. Lo and behold, the chipmunk didn't want the peanut after all; he just wanted the fun of the chase.

Presumably, there will be no chipmunks under these Tall Pine Trees. This pattern should be made into a quilt—a big project, but worth the perseverance. The number of patches used will determine the size of the quilt. Each patch is 14 inches square.

Materials

The quantities given will make a quilt measuring 56 inches by 70 inches with no borders. For a larger quilt or one with borders, add additional fabric.

    7 yards main color (MC) for top patches, back, and binding
    2¼ yards contrasting color (CC)
    Batting
    ¼-inch-wide masking tape

Cut, for Quilt

    Two pieces 72 inches long by 29 inches wide for back
    7¼ yards bias binding
    Cut, for each patch
    Two #1 MC rectangles
    One #2 MC rectangles

    Two #3 MC triangles
    Two #4 MC triangles
    Two #5 MC triangles
    Four #3 CC triangles
    Four #4 CC triangles

Making the Tall Pine Tree Patch

1. Make the top half first. Start by stitching a #3 CC and a #4 CC triangle to either side of a #5 triangle (see diagram 1). Make two of these.

2. Sew these two pieces together, having the point of one MC triangle at the center of the long side of the other MC triangle (refer to diagram 2).

3. Now, add a #1 rectangle to either side of the unit made in step 2 (diagram 3). This completes the top half.

4. To make the bottom half of the square, stitch a #3 triangle to a #4 triangle (diagram 4). Make four of these.

5. Sew two of these units together (see diagram 5). Repeat this step with the other two units, making sure that they are the mirror images of the first two units.

6. Stitch one of these sections to each side of the #2 rectangle (diagram 6).

7. Finally, stitch the top and bottom halves of the square together to form the completed patch.

Assembling the Quilt

For a quilt, just stitch complete patches together until you have the number needed. (Add a border, if desired.)

1. To prepare the quilt back, stitch the two backing pieces together vertically, using a ½-inch seam allowance.

2. Lay the prepared quilt back wrong-side up on the floor. Spread the quilt batting on top of this. Finally, lay the pieced Tall Pine Tree top face-up on the batting. Baste through all layers. Do a good amount of basting, always starting at the center and working toward the outside edge.

3. It is time to quilt. Use a hoop and start in the quilt center. Outline quilt around the triangles, using the masking tape as a guide. Transfer the quilting pattern to the large MC triangles and quilt. (If your quilt includes a border, work a quilting pattern of your choice on the border area.)

4. After the quilting has been completed, trim the back and batting the same size as the top. Prepare the MC bias binding as described on page 14. Stitch the binding around the entire quilt using a blind stitch.

MC   *CC*

Diagram 1

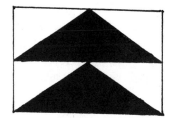

Diagram 2

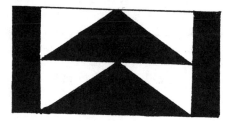

Diagram 3

Diagram 4

Diagram 5

Diagram 6

Completed Square

#2

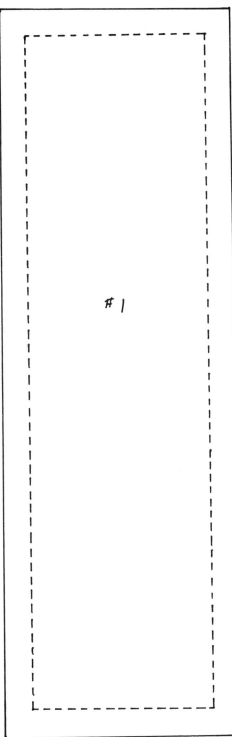

#1

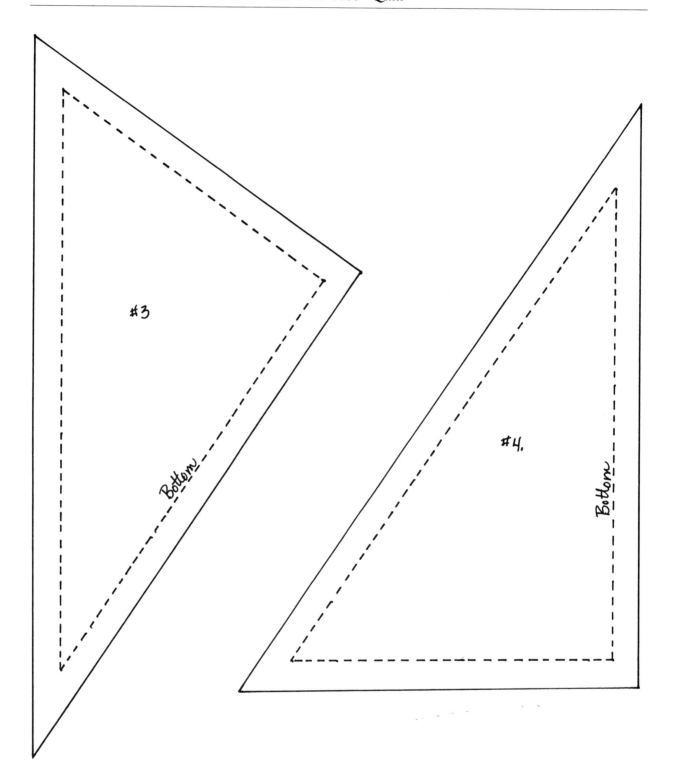

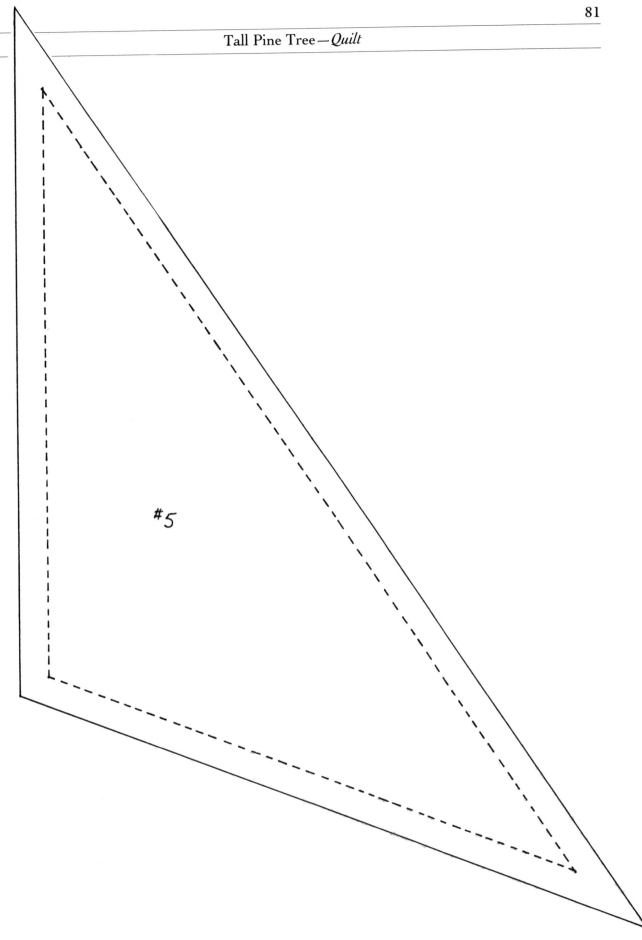

#5

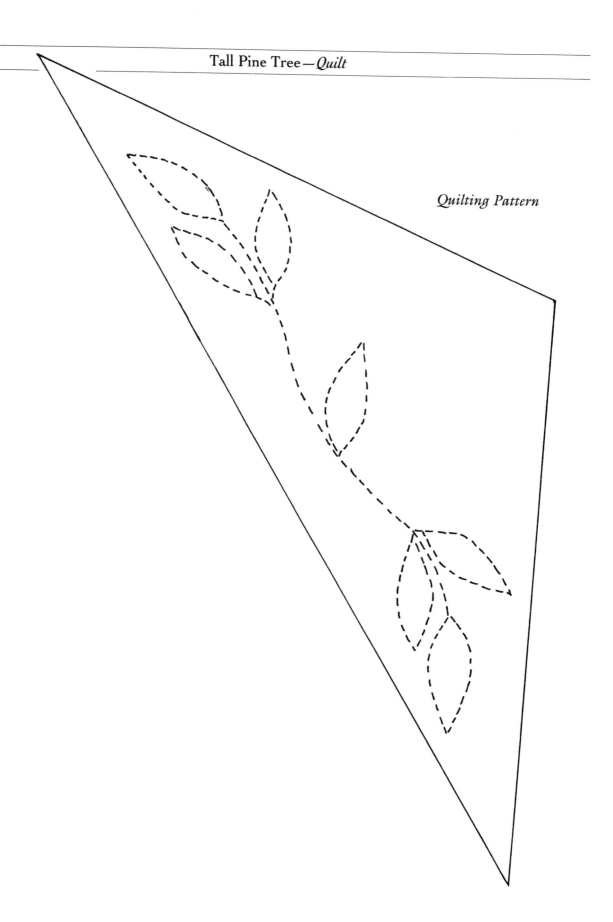

Quilting Pattern

BOUNCING BUOYS

Our friend, Mr. Webster, lists "boi" as the first pronunciation for the word *buoy*. Any fisherman will tell you that is the land-lubber's version. According to anyone raised along the coast of Maine, the second dictionary listing is the correct and only way to say the word. Natives say "boo´ee."

Dictionaries are excellent publications. They tell us how to spell a word, how to pronounce it, what part of speech it is, and the exact meaning or meanings. Teachers rely on dictionaries for several functions, including those just listed.

Our number five child, David, is old enough now to start confessing his childhood transgressions. One he owned up to recently was the fact that he is a cutup in school. No surprise. Why should he behave differently in school than anywhere else? He had too much energy to sit still for more than a few minutes. I used to tell my friends that if he had been my first-born, he would be an only child.

But I digress.

As previously stated, teachers have many uses for dictionaries. David's fourth-grade teacher used one for "dictionary pages." This stratagem was employed when a student did not conduct himself appropriately. The pupil was required to sit quietly and copy dictionary pages.

It seems my son transcribed his way so far into Mr. Webster's lexicon that the little rascal became known as Dictionary Dave.

I am certain of two things concerning Dave. One is that he was born an imp and will go out the same way. The second is that, with or without a dictionary, he calls a buoy a "boo´ee."

These Bouncing Buoy bibs will bounce from table to washer and dryer with no problems. The full-size bibs are great fun for lobster dinners or even for spaghetti feeds. I also include a version for the small fry.

Materials

The adult size is 15 inches wide by 21 inches long
The junior version is 8 inches wide by 9 inches long

    1⅜ yards fabric for four large and one (or more) small bibs
    1⅜ yards muslin for backs
    ⅛ yard for traps
    Scraps for trap ends, buoys, and buoy trims
    Batting
    12 yards bias tape

Cut

    Four large bib fronts—and small bib front(s), if desired. (See step 1.)
    Four large muslin bib backs—and small back(s), if desired
    Trap and trap end appliqué pieces, one set per bib
    One buoy appliqué piece per bib, using a variety of fabrics
    Trim for buoys

Making the Bouncing Buoys Bibs

1. Using a large paper bag, make the pattern for the large bib. Cut a portion of the bag to measure 15 inches by 21 inches. Fold in half lengthwise. Place the pattern for bib top at one end of the bag with the dotted line against the fold. Transfer the markings.

Now, place the bottom of the pattern at the other end of the bag with the dotted line against the fold and transfer those markings. Connect the lines to make one continuous outer edge. Cut around the marked outline.

Unfold the paper pattern and pin it to the fabric. Cut. Next, cut the backs from muslin using the same paper pattern.

2. Make templates for the buoys, buoy trim, trap, and trap end. Trace these onto the chosen fabric. Cut out the pieces, adding a one-eighth-inch seam allowance all around each piece.

3. Following the appliqué directions in the "Appliqué? Absolutely!" chapter (page 15), stitch the pieces in place on the bibs.

4. Transfer wave quilting pattern from the Seashells project (page 34) to each bib.

5. Make a sandwich of the appliquéd bib top, batting, and the muslin back. Baste.

6. Quilt closely around the outline of the lobster trap and buoy. Quilt the trap, following the lines on the pattern. Quilt the "waves."

7. Starting at the neck edge, stitch bias tape around the outside of the bib. End at the opposite

neck edge. Cut the bias even with the edge.

Leaving a 12-inch tail at the beginning, stitch bias around the bib neck. Leave another 12-inch tail at the end.

The bibs are now ready for the test. Serve a lobster or spaghetti feast, don the bibs, and see how clean they keep you. If you soil your sleeve, you're on your own.

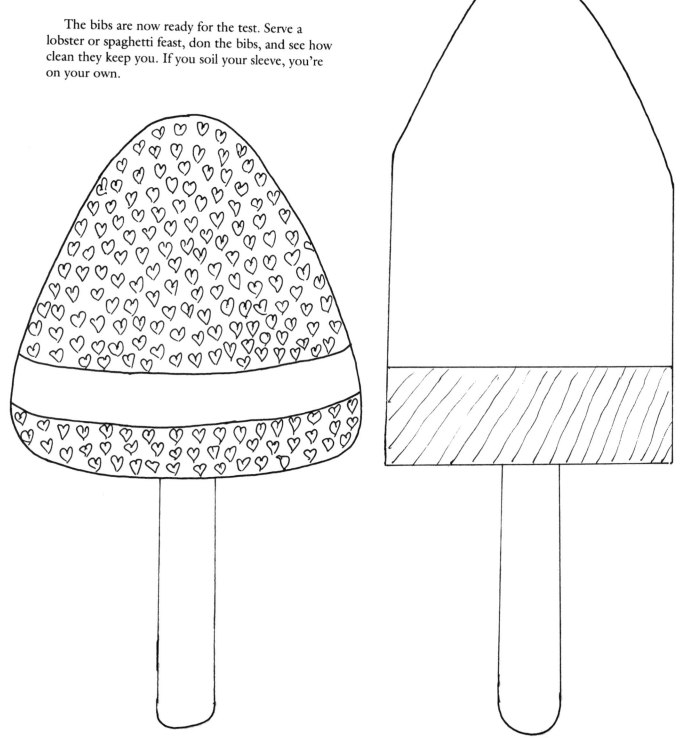

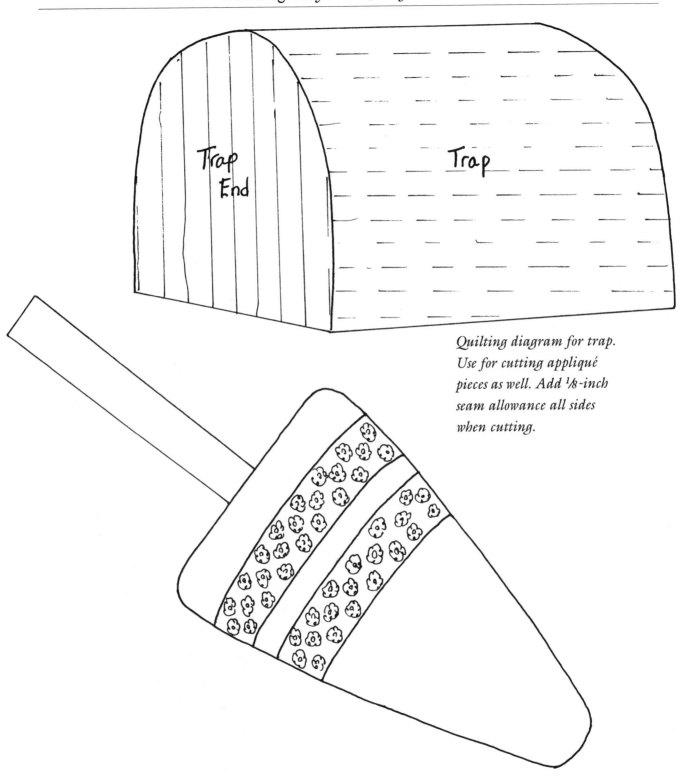

Quilting diagram for trap. Use for cutting appliqué pieces as well. Add ⅛-inch seam allowance all sides when cutting.

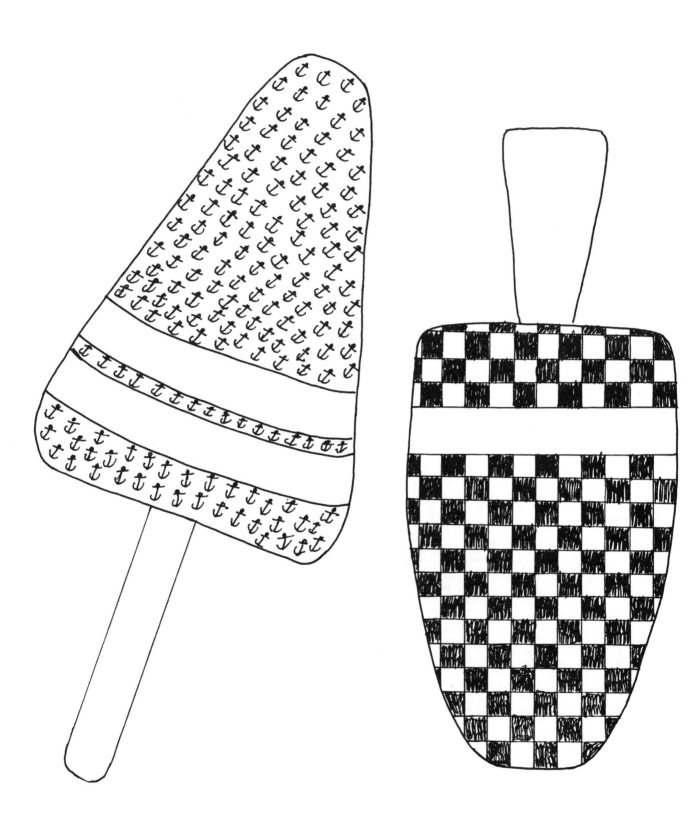

This is half of the small bib pattern. Place broken line on fold of fabric and cut through double thickness.

Place on fold

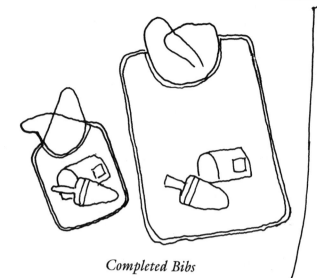

Completed Bibs

Large Bib, Top Portion

Large Bib, Bottom Portion

LOBSTERBOATS

Lobstermen are a breed apart from the rest of us. They are independent, hard-working and, in most cases, extremely easygoing.

I suppose they have to be all of these things to survive. To an outsider it seems a glamorous occupation—a life of sun and sea. In reality it is a hard life. The instability of the market and uncertainties of the lobster population make the business unpredictable. But most of all, there is the unreliability of the weather. To be sure, lobstermen do not have to ride out storms at sea. They do, however, have to sit and look wistfully at the sky, wondering when they will be able to haul again.

And it is not a sunny-day job. When lobstermen are not out hauling traps, they have equipment to maintain, buoys to paint, and various other chores to do.

Lobstering does have its compensations. How many jobs start the day with a beautiful sunrise? Then there is that unmistakable bond between man and nature. And there are those occasional perfect days of sun and sea.

Many people would trade their jobs for something else, but this is not true of lobstermen. Ask any lobster fisherman if he loves his work, and his simple answer will be, "Ayuh!"

Materials

The overall size of this wallhanging is 29 inches by 29 inches.

⅝ yards fabric for sky
1½ yards fabric for sea, backing, and binding
⅛ yard calico for lobster traps
13-by-6-inch piece calico for large lobster boat
15-by-6-inch piece calico for wharf section
Scraps for small boats, trap ends, pot buoy, boat windows
Batting

Cut

One 29-inch-square piece for backing
One 16-by-29-inch piece for sky
One 13-by-29-inch piece for sea
One large lobster boat; cut pieces a, b, and c separately
Three small lobster boats; cut each as one piece
Three lobster traps

Three lobster trap ends
One buoy
One wharf section
One large boat window
Three small boat windows

Making the Wall Hanging

1. Using a half-inch seam, stitch the sky and sea together along a long edge.

2. Make templates for each pattern piece and trace them onto the chosen fabric. Cut the parts out, adding a one-eighth-inch seam allowance all around each piece.

3. Following the appliqué direction in the "Appliqué? Absolutely!" chapter (page 15), baste the pieces in place on the background. Blind-stitch around each piece. Cut a 6-inch piece of bias tape and stitch it at the back of the large boat for a mast.

4. Transfer the wave quilting design to the sea section of the hanging.

5. Make a sandwich of the back, batting, and the appliquéd top. Baste.

6. Quilt the hanging. Quilt close to each appliquéd piece first. Then quilt along the wave pattern lines. Quilt the sky any way you choose.

7. Make bias binding and stitch it around the outside of the hanging.

8. Attach rings to the hanging back just below the top edge. This will allow you to display the work easily.

Completed Wall Hanging

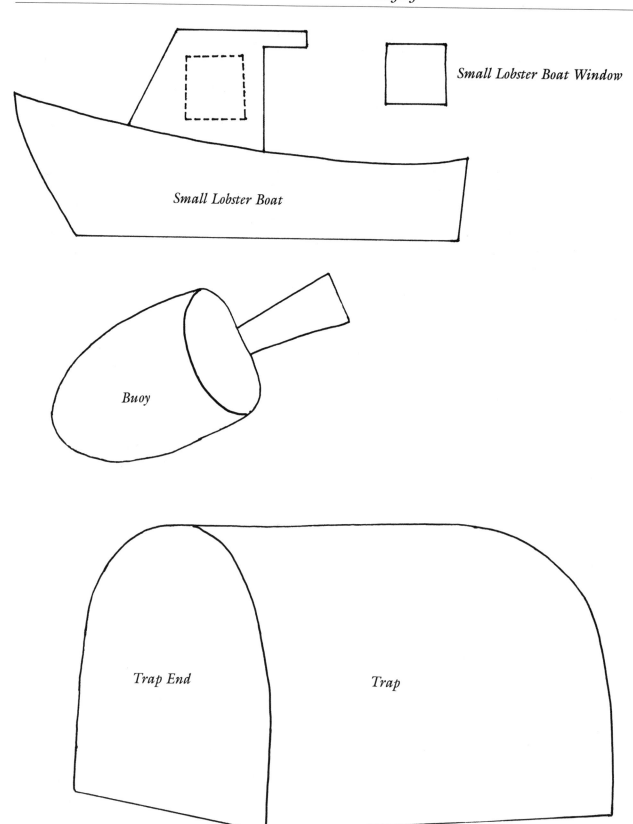

Small Lobster Boat Window

Small Lobster Boat

Buoy

Trap End

Trap

Lobsterboats — *Wall Hanging*

Wave Quilting Design

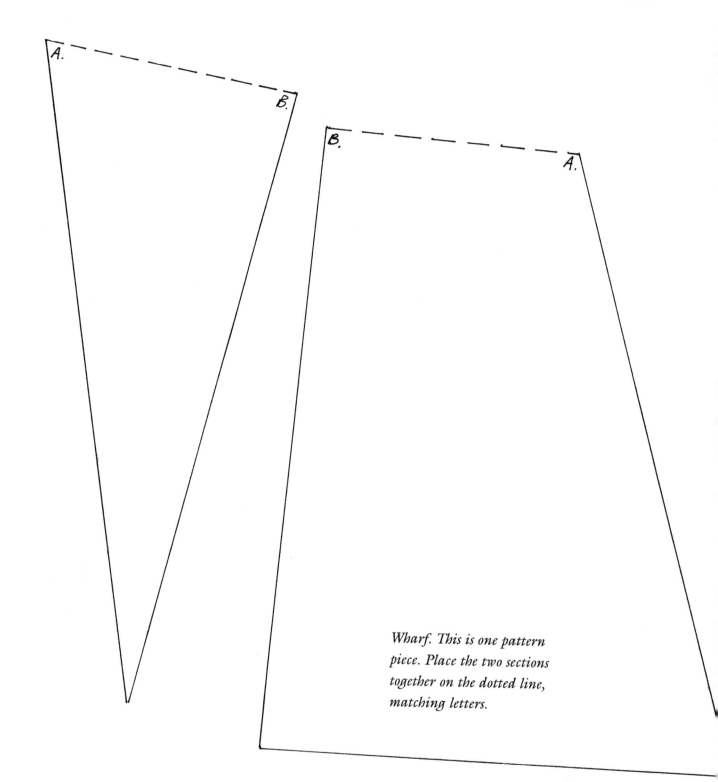

Wharf. This is one pattern
piece. Place the two sections
together on the dotted line,
matching letters.

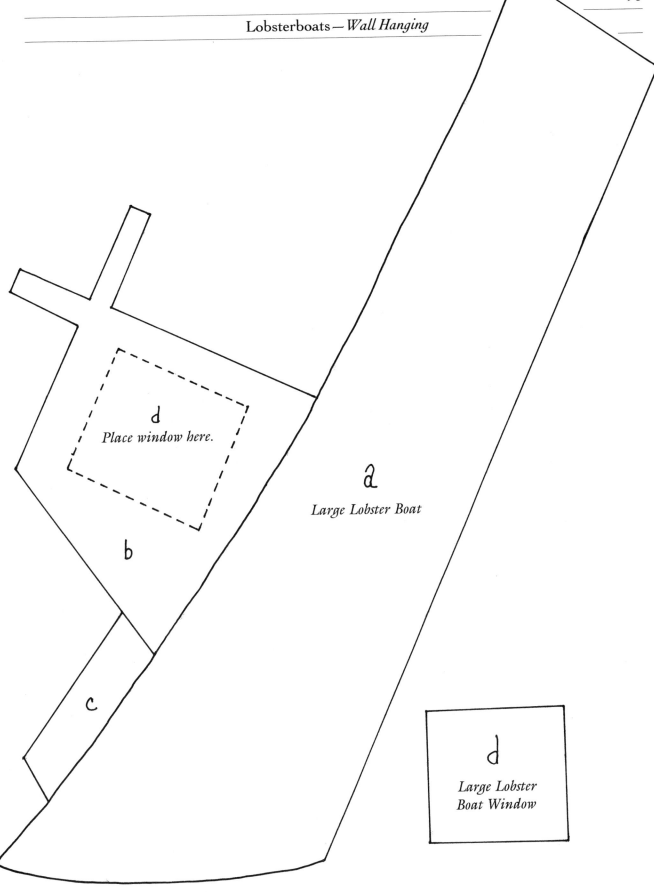

d

Place window here.

b

c

a

Large Lobster Boat

d

Large Lobster Boat Window

DELECTABLE MOUNTAINS

When we moved to our present home, we purchased a great old farmhouse. Unfortunately, after a couple of years the shed needed replacing. Our oldest son, Tim, assured his father that between the two of them it would be a relatively easy undertaking.

The work had progressed to the point of shingling the roof when one morning my terrific son appeared in my kitchen and announced that he was going to shingle the shed roof and would need *my* help. I panicked. I pleaded. I do not like heights and was sure I could not get from a ladder to the roof. Tim stood his ground. He needed me, and there was no changing his mind.

To make a long story short, he coaxed me onto the roof and then told me we would be starting at the edge. At this time I became physically ill.

I said, "I can't do this. I'm sorry."

My son looked me square in the eye and without flinching informed me that he was not going to listen to talk like that from a woman who had spent years telling him there was no such word as *can't*.

Needless to say, the roof got shingled, and I was thankful that Tim had been so unyielding. How else would I have known that the low mountains near our home are delectable when viewed from twenty-plus feet in the air?

This wall hanging features a row of mountains encircling a star. To make it larger, just keep adding rows of mountains.

Materials

The wall hanging is 34 inches square, including a 4½-inch border.

  1¼ yards main color (MC)
  1½ yards contrasting color (CC)
  Batting
  ¼-inch-wide masking tape

Cut

  One 35-by-35-inch CC square for back
  Two 25-inch by 4½-inch MC border strips
  Two 34-inch by 4½-inch MC border strips
  Eight #1 MC parallelograms
  Four #4 MC trapezoids, then flip template face-down and cut four more

Four #5 MC trapezoids, then flip template face-down and cut four more
Four #6 MC trapezoids, then flip template face-down and cut four more
Eight #2 CC triangles
Eight #3 CC triangles
Sixteen #7 CC triangles
Four #8 CC triangles
Four #9 CC squares
Four CC 13-by-13-by-18½-inch triangles
Four yards MC bias binding (page 14 gives instructions for making your own bias binding)

Making the Wall Hanging

1. Make the center star square first. Stitch a #2 triangle to a short side of a #1 parallelogram. Then stitch the long side of a #3 triangle to a long side of the parallelogram to form a triangle. (See diagram 1.) Repeat this procedure seven more times. Note that 4 of the triangle units are mirror images of the others.

2. Next, stitch two of these triangles together to form a square (diagram 2). Make four of these squares.

3. Sew two squares together to make a rectangle, as in diagram 3. Repeat once more.

4. Stitch these rectangles together to form the center star square, following diagram 4. Set aside.

5. Stitch one short side of a #7 triangle to the top (slanted side) of each #5 and #6 trapezoid. Next, stitch a #4 trapezoid to a #5. Then add a #6 trapezoid to this (diagram 5). Make eight of these. Remember, four will face one way and four will face the other way. Each of these constitutes a "trapezoid section."

6. Stitch one side of a #9 square to the top of a #4 trapezoid. Repeat three more times (diagram 6).

7. Sew each trapezoid section with square attached to a section without a square. Start stitching at the bottom of the sections and continue up, stitching the other side of the square to the top of the other #4 piece. (See diagram 7.) Repeat this step three more times. There are now four completed mountain sections.

8. Attach mountain sections to opposite sides of the center star square. Set aside.

9. Stitch a #8 triangle to each end of the other

two mountain sections (diagram 8).

10. Now, sew these mountain sections to the remaining two sides of the center star square.

11. Sew a large 13-inch triangle to each side of this patch.

12. Add a border strip to each side of the completed top, mitering the corners.

13. Make a sandwich of the back, batting, and the Delectable Mountains top. Baste.

14. Quilt the center star and the mountains with outline quilting, using the masking tape as a guide.

15. In each corner triangle, use the large and small star-quilting designs (or a design of your choice). These star patterns were copied from two antique tin templates. The small star is somewhat askew, but that adds a certain charm to the design.

16. Transfer the leaf design around the border and quilt. You will be able to fit five leaves along each side. Quilt three acorns in each corner.

17. Trim the back and batting even with the top. Sew binding around the outside edge. Attach rings to the back for ease in hanging.

MC   CC

Diagram 1   *Diagram 2*   *Diagram 3*

Diagram 4   *Diagram 5*

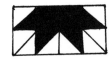

Diagram 6

Diagram 7

Diagram 8

Completed Wall Hanging

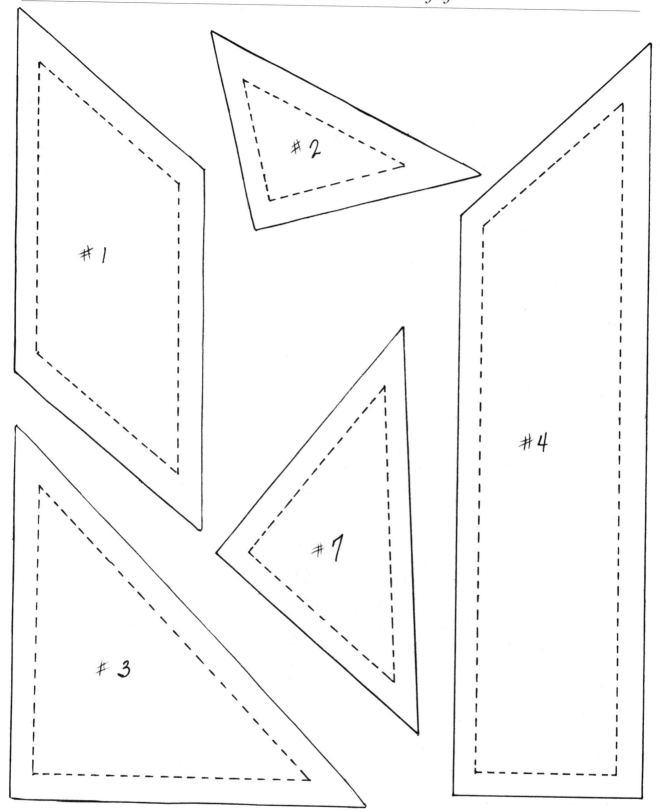

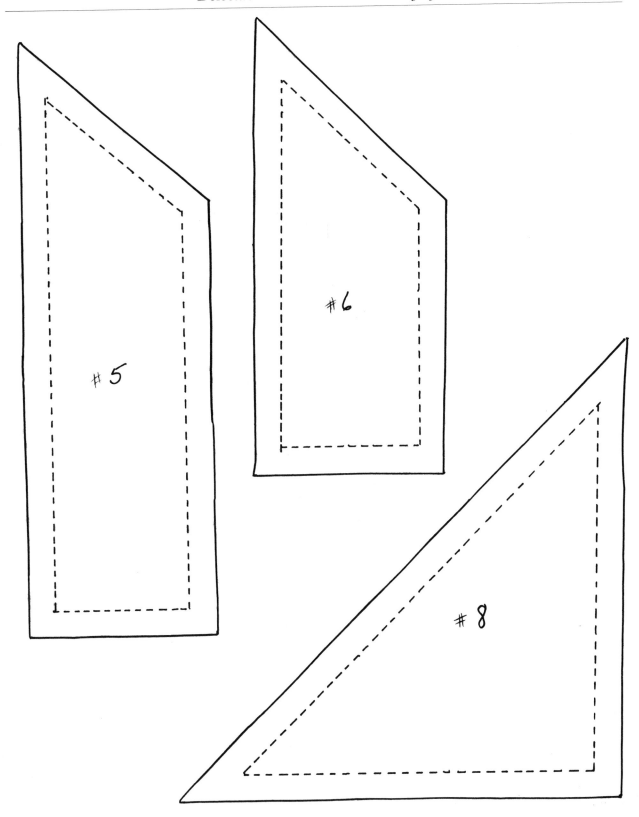

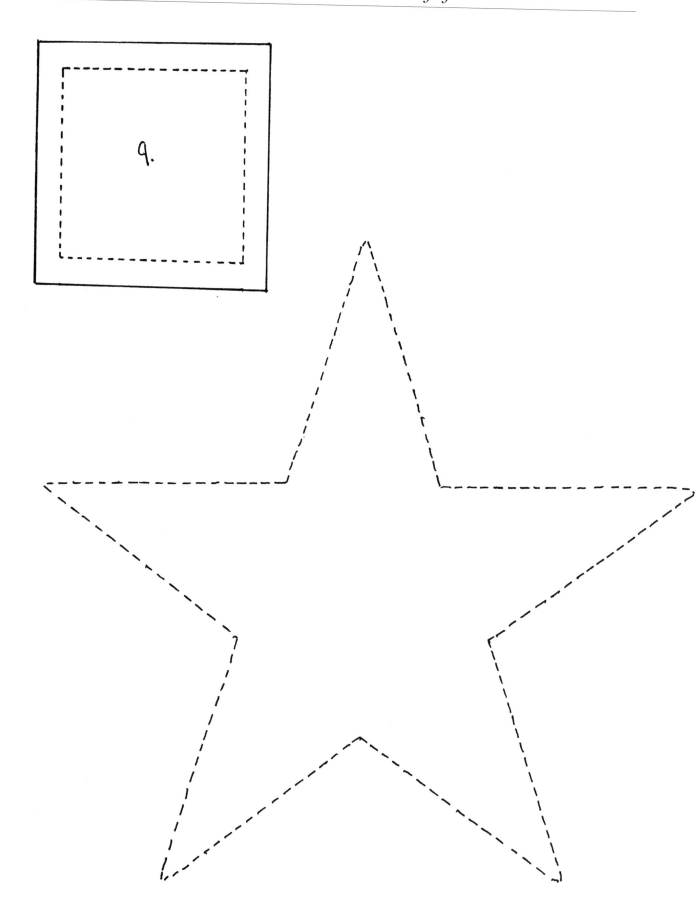

9.

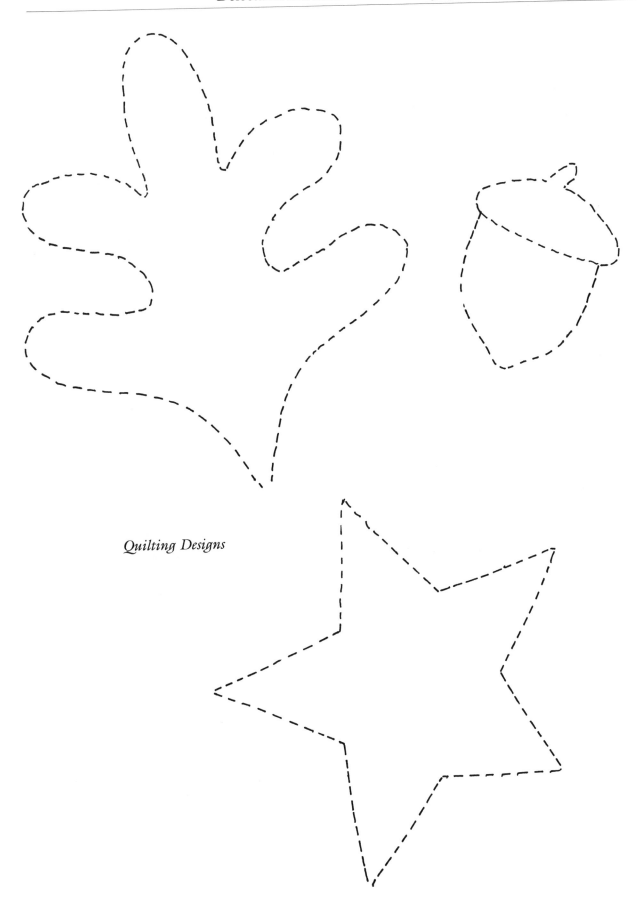

Quilting Designs

STORMBOUND

I remember one January morning as a child, waking to a full-blown snowstorm. There obviously was not going to be school that day, but convincing my mother of that fact was another matter. She put my breakfast on the table as usual and made me go through the whole routine of brushing teeth, scrubbing behind my ears, and getting bundled up in ninety-two layers of clothing. My mother believed in dressing me warmly, even though it meant I was completely helpless if I slipped and fell. Since the schoolhouse was only "down the hill" from our house, she allowed as how it would not hurt me to go and make sure that school had indeed been canceled.

When I was all ready, with scarf adjusted so I could barely see where I was, let alone where I was going, she tried to open the outside door. Well, the snow had blown and drifted up against the door, and no amount of pushing and shoving was going to budge it.

We were stormbound. I was in heaven, but my mother muttered all day about my missing a day of school.

This wall hanging represents a stormy scene, with white snow and patches of gray sky surrounding red chimneys. The quilting design swirls around the patches as if being driven by a bitter wind. This project is a little more time-consuming than many of the others in this book, but the end result is well worth the effort. It looks equally lovely hanging on a wall, covering a table, or draped over a chair.

Materials

The overall size of this hanging is 47 inches by 47 inches.

2½ yards main color (MC) fabric
1½ yards white contrasting (WC) fabric
1 yard red contrasting (RC) fabric
Batting
¼-inch-wide masking tape

Cut

Two 48-by-24½-inch pieces MC for the back
Thirty-two #1 MC squares
Forty #2 MC triangles
Thirty #1 WC squares
Eighty #2 WC triangles
Eight #3 WC squares
Thirty #1 RC squares
Thirty-two #2 RC triangles
One #3 RC square
Four #4 RC squares
Four 3-by-35½-inch WC strips
Four 3½-by-41-inch MC strips

Piecing Together the Top

To avoid confusion as you construct this complex design, follow the directions step by step and consult the finished-square diagram as you work each step. It will also help to lay out the entire square on a flat surface. Returning the pieces to their proper places as you finish stitching them.

1. Make forty squares by stitching forty #2 MC and forty #2 WC triangles together.

2. Make thirty-two squares from #2 RC and #2 WC triangles together.

3. Make four squares by stitching two #2 WC triangles together.

4. Now, by stitching together two of the MC and WC squares formed in step 1, make twenty rectangles (see diagram 1). These will be referred to as M/W rectangles.

5. As in step 4, make sixteen rectangles by stitching together two RC and WC squares that were formed in step 2. These will be referred to as R/W rectangles.

6. Make the center square of the hanging by sewing a M/W rectangle to opposite sides of the #3 RC square, with the NC side against the RC square.

Next, using the WC squares made from pairs of #2 WC triangles, stitch one square to each short side of another M/W rectangle. Repeat this once more.

Now, stitch these two longer rectangles to the other two sides of the RC square section. (See diagram 2.)

7. Make a star patch section by piecing together a #3 WC square with two R/W rectangles on opposite sides, with the WC side against the WC square.

Then stitch #1 MC squares to both ends of a M/W rectangle. Repeat once more. Sew these strips to the other two sides of the WC square section. (See diagram 3.) Make three more stars in this manner.

8. Make a star patch by piecing together a #3 WC square with one R/W rectangle and one M/W

rectangle on opposite sides.

Stitch a #1 RC square to one end and a #1 MC square to the other end of an M/W rectangle. Sew this to one of the remaining sides of the WC square section.

Next, stitch #1 MC squares to both ends of a R/W rectangle. Sew this to the remaining side of the WC square section. Make three more stars in this manner. See diagram 4.

9. Following diagram 5, make a row with three star patches. The middle star should have four MC corner patches. The others should each have one RC corner. Make another row exactly the same way.

10. Stitch the remaining two star patches (they should both have four MC corner squares) to opposite ends of the center square made in step 6 (see diagram 6).

11. Now, positioning the row from step 10 in the middle, stitch these three rows together, completing the large star square.

12. Make two long strips with alternating RC #1 and WC #1 squares. There will be 12 squares in each strip, six RC and six WC. Sew one of these strips to one side of the large star square, having a RC at the top. Then, stitch the other strip to the opposite side of the large square, having a WC square at the top.

13. Make two more strips using the remaining #1 RC and WC squares. Each strip will have seven squares of each color, for a total of fourteen squares.

Now, stitch these to the two remaining sides of the large star square, having one with a WC square at the beginning and the other side with a RC square. See the finished-square diagram.

14. Stitch WC strips to opposite sides of the large star square. Sew a #1 MC square to each end of the other two long WC strips. Sew these strips to the remaining sides of the large star square.

15. Then sew MC strips to opposite sides of the large star square. Stitch a #4 RC square to each end of the other two MC strips. Finally, sew these to the remaining sides of the large square. (Your Stormbound top is finished—take a break!)

Assembling the Wall Hanging

1. Using a half-inch seam, stitch the two backing pieces together, forming a 48-inch square.

2. Make a sandwich of the Stormbound top, batting, and the backing square. Baste.

3. Quilt the entire top. Use quilting pattern #1 for the star sections. Have the middle of the quilting pattern centered in the large WC center squares of the stars and also in the RC center square of the top.

Outline quilt around each #1 square, using masking tape as a guide.

Transfer the #2 quilting pattern to the WC and MC strips portion and quilt.

4. After the quilting has been completed, make bias binding (see page 14) and sew it around the outside edge.

MC   WC   RC

Diagram 1

Diagram 2

Diagram 3   *Diagram 4*

Diagram 5

Completed Wall Hanging

Diagram 6

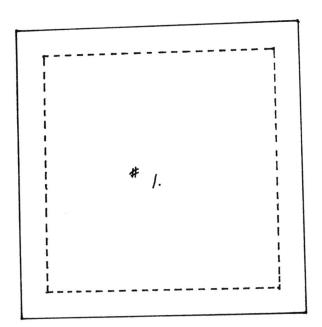

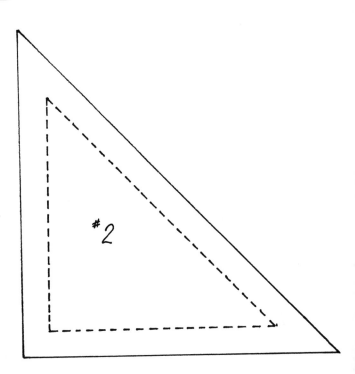

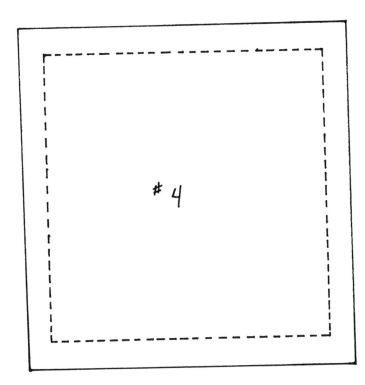

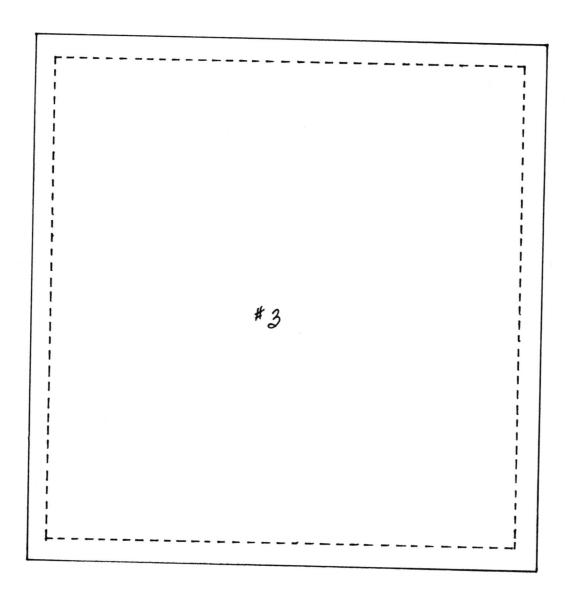

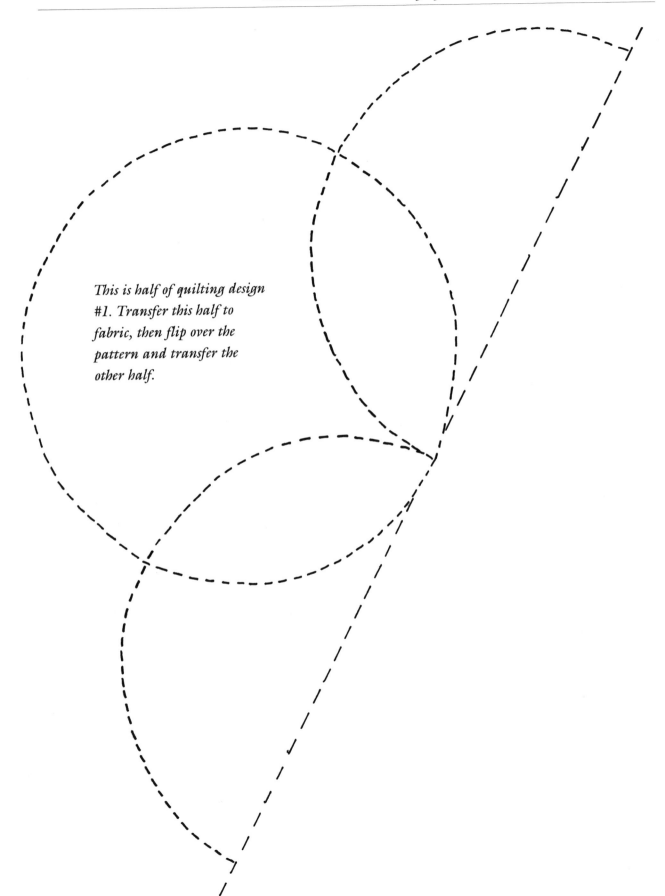

This is half of quilting design #1. Transfer this half to fabric, then flip over the pattern and transfer the other half.

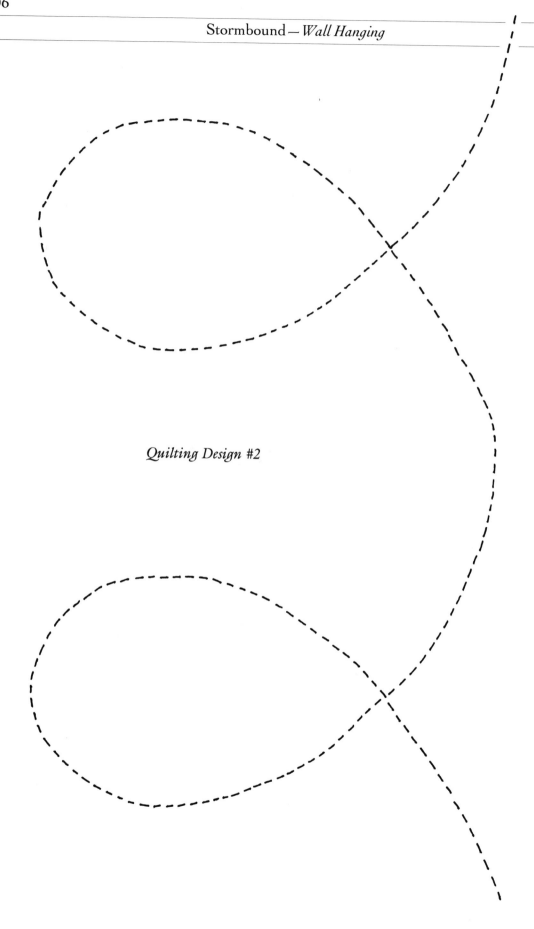

Quilting Design #2

PERKY PATCHWORK PICNIC SET

I cannot begin to remember all the times we've been on picnics. It still remains my favorite thing to do in the summer. We always celebrate Independence Day by attending the Portland Symphony's outdoor concert. We take a picnic lunch and enjoy the total atmosphere. Each year as we're departing, I'm ready to do it again the next day.

I've even been on a few winter picnics. They are a little chilly, but fun nonetheless. One winter, we picnicked every other week. We would go grocery shopping and then park by the waterfront and have a picnic in the car. It was cold outside, but nothing could match the warmth inside. The kids loved it (we had two at that time).

Picnics may be plain or fancy. They may feature lobster or peanut butter. The object of a picnic is not the food but being outside to relax and forget the everyday problems that plague us all.

This perky cloth and napkins set will brighten any picnic. Just add food and ants.

Materials

The picnic cloth measures 44 inches by 44 inches. Napkins (made of CC) measure 15 inches square.
  3 yards main color (MC)
  1¾ yards contrasting color (CC)
  Batting
  ¼-inch-wide masking tape

Cut for Picnic Cloth

  44-by-44-inch MC square for cloth top
  44-by-44-inch MC square for cloth back
  Four 11-by-11-by-15½-inch MC triangles
  180 inches of CC bias binding

Cut for <u>Each</u> Lobster Patch

  Thirty #1 MC squares
  Twelve #2 MC triangles
  Two #3 MC triangles
  Two #4 MC triangles
  Four #1 CC squares
  Twelve #2 CC triangles
  Four #3 CC triangles
  One #4 CC triangle
  Six #5 CC lobster legs for appliqué, adding ⅛ inch
    seam allowance

Making the Lobster Patch

1. Stitch a #2 MC triangle to a #2 CC triangle to form a square (see diagram 1). Make twelve of these squares.

2. Stitch a #3 CC triangle to each side of a #4 MC triangle twice (diagram 2).

3. Sew a #3 MC triangle to each side of the #4 CC triangle—same arrangement as in step 2 above.

4. Following the lobster diagram, assemble the squares into 7 rows. (These rows will consist of plain squares and the squares formed in steps 1 through 3.) then sew together the rows to make the completed lobster patch.

5. Appliqué the legs to the lobster sides. (I know; lobsters have four legs per side, but I took artistic license with this design. Just think what a great conversation piece it will make.)

Embroider eyes and antennae.

6. Attach an 11-by-11-by-15½-inch triangle to two sides of a lobster square. (See diagram 3.) Repeat with the other patch.

7. Make a second lobster patch following the above steps.

Assembling the Picnic Cloth

1. Measure and mark one side 23 inches from the corner of the MC top cloth. Repeat on the adjoining side. Draw a line from mark to mark. Cut this triangular piece from the cloth. (See diagram 4.) Repeat this on the opposite corner.

2. Cut a 7½-by-7½-by-10-inch triangle from remaining two corners (see diagram 5). Repeat steps 1 and 2 on the picnic cloth back.

3. Using a quarter-inch seam, stitch the lobster sections to the cloth in place of the corners cut off in step 1 above.

4. Make a sandwich of the back, batting, and the completed top. Baste.

5. Outline quilt around each square of the lobster patch, using the masking tape as a guide.

6. Transfer the wave quilting design from the Silent Sentinel pattern (page 61) or the Lobsterboats pattern (page 91) to the rest of the picnic cloth. Quilt along these lines.

6. Prepare bias binding as described on page 14. Finish the picnic cloth by stitching binding around the outside.

Making the Napkins

1. Pull a thread across the fabric to ensure a straight cutting line.

2. Cut four napkins measuring 15½ inches by 15½ inches each.

3. Press under ¼ inch around the napkin. Press under ¼ inch once more. Hem the napkin.

4. Repeat with the other three.

MC   CC

Diagram 1   *Diagram 2*

Diagram 3

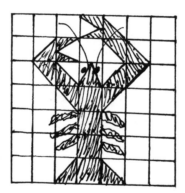

Completed Lobster Patch

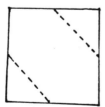 

Diagram 4   *Diagram 5*

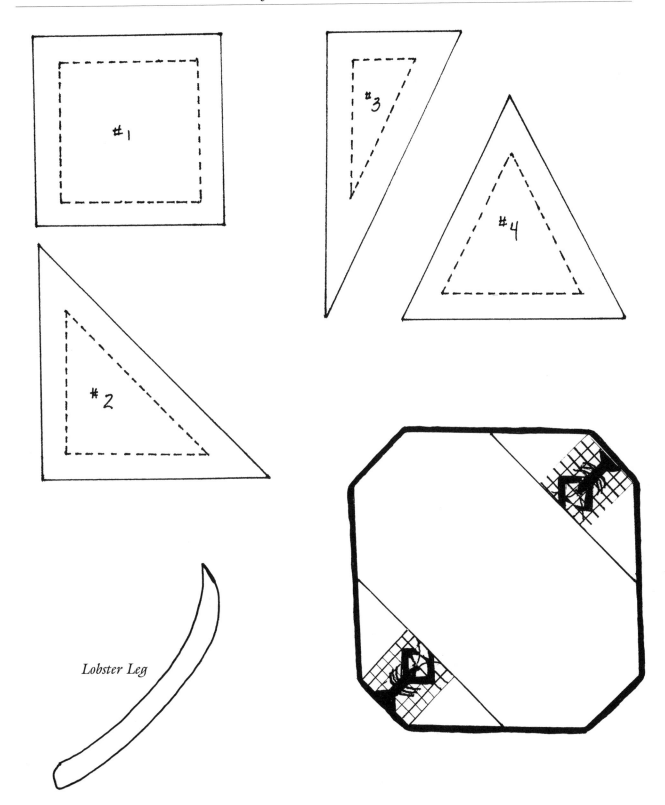

#1

#3

#4

#2

Lobster Leg